Big!

World Records in the Streets!
plus
Tap Dancing Galore

Beth Obermeyer

NORTH STAR PRESS OF ST. CLOUD, INC.
St. Cloud, Minnesota

Dedicated
to the one I love

Cover art: Annie Scheumbauer

Copyright © 2011 Mary Beth Obermeyer

ISBN-13: 978-0-87839-437-1

All rights reserved.

First Edition, August 2011

Printed in the United States of America

Published by
North Star Press of St. Cloud, Inc.
P.O. Box 451
St. Cloud, Minnesota 56302

www.northstarpress.com

BIG!

Table of Contents

Prologue vi

Part I: Solos:
The Backbeat

Chapter 1	Tapping the Nutcracker: My Favorite Celebrity	3
Chapter 2	At the Governor's Mansion—on Christmas Eve	11
Chapter 3	Garrison Keillor: *A Prairie Home Companion*	13
Chapter 4	Christopher Plummer: *The British Series*; Minnesota Orchestra	19
Chapter 5	The *Tap-Dance Concerto* Tours with the Minnesota Orchestra	24
Chapter 6	Paul Draper: the Tap-Dancer's Tap Dancer	28
Chapter 7	Gregory Hines: Dancer, Singer, Actor	33
Chapter 8	Eleanor Powell, Film Star, 1935-1945	39
Chapter 9	Big Bird	48
Chapter 10	The Doughboy	49
Chapter 11	On Air and on Paper	51
Chapter 12	The Flanagan Phenomenon: Going Boldface in Barbara	53

Part II
Record Breakers Take the Town

Chapter 13	Finding the Way	59
Chapter 14	The Big Tap: The World's Largest Tap Dance	65
Chapter 15	The World's Longest Bucket Brigade	67
Chapter 16	The World's Largest Marching Band	79
Chapter 17	The Great Shake	91
Chapter 18	The World's Longest Tap Dance	94
Chapter 19	The World's Longest Chorus Line	97
Chapter 20	Leapfrogging in Frogtown	101
Chapter 21	The Mass Break Dance	104
Chapter 22	The First Minnesota Festival of the Book	108
Epilogue		110
Out-Takes and Hind-Sights		115

Prologue

Remember, that Once Upon A Time? The day we . . .
The stuff was magic, all those world records, set by the people, on the streets they cared about—the busiest ones. Everyone pulled together, everyone.

The events began with the uprising of 1,801 tap dancers, who opened their arts center, into the *Guinness Book of World Records*. Soon an enormous marching band came along, "like a giant segmented insect holding the city under a siege of sound," said Ann Braatas, *St. Paul Pioneer Press*. And five more spectaculars: a six-mile bucket brigade, a chorus line, a mass break dance, even leapfrogging. Always, the arms waved, the bodies turned and heads bobbed, to infinity. The people practiced hard at being together, and found in the process that they were much more alike than different—all with so much coverage one wondered if a war had been declared.

But organizing those big events took courage. I had to let go of certainties, take risks, on big streets. Understandably, in between, I danced—had to—the backbeat of my life, since forever.

But my solos were never quite where one would think, either: a runway, the bib of the stage at Orchestra Hall, on national radio, atop a water fountain. I tap-danced with Gregory Hines, alongside Christopher Plummer,

Garrison Keillor. Big Bird, the Doughboy. In the governor's solarium on Christmas Eve, as the Nutcracker. They were celebrities all, ones I never thought I'd meet, in places I never thought tap would go.

And that is my story: our *World Records in the Streets. Plus Tap Dancing Galore*. It was quality hoopla in Whoville—all that passion and exuberance.

Except this is no tale. The story is real because do we have Out-Takes!

My story starts with a solo. It's an ordinary evening, a stroll into the lobby of the Minnesota Dance Theatre, back to the business of teaching, just three weeks after the Big Tap.

Turn up the music! The year is 1979.

Part I
Solos: The Backbeat

1

Tapping the Nutcracker
My Favorite Celebrity

A silver invitation caught the low afternoon sunlight, a sparkle amidst schedules and flyers, on the board in the lobby, the Minnesota Dance Theatre. I didn't care, not one bit, not even about the red-velvet dancer on its shiny face. Someone else somewhere was organizing this one. I clicked past Lynn the registrar with a smile, on the way to the elevator.

He tipped his head, his blue eyes on me. I knew the look.

Land mine ahead.

Nuh uh, was what I said to myself. I've got nothing on top of me for the next month but Christmas. The 1,801 tap dancers went home weeks ago, happy with their world record, set on our Hennepin Avenue. But something about the glint off that mirror card on the board pulled.

"The Tapping Nutcracker," was what the invitation shouted, from five feet away. The red dancer on the card—it tap-danced like a fairy.

I stopped breathing, let my bag slide to my . . . tap toes.

Mr. Bourman, the school director, popped out his doorway. He came to my side.

"Mr. Bourman! What is this?" I asked.

Opposite: Tapping Nutcracker, Beth. (Darlene Pfister. *Minneapolis Star* photo. Used with permission)

The man paled, almost as white as his gauze sleeves.

"Mary Beth, if you don't know—I am uncertain who might."

I'd been through it with Mr. Bourman. He'd arrived, the new school director, just two months ago, to find his only tap teacher, me, recruiting tap dancers from the street, the workplace, the churches. I'd even had my eye on his Performing Arts children, to open our arts center. After shocked beginnings, we'd found common ground, and we'd become best allies. He'd even toted chairs to the registration spot for the Big Tap, a gravel parking lot nearby. But I wasn't, I didn't, I would never push my luck.

"I'm doing a six-mile bucket brigade next, Mr. Bourman. They just reach for a bucket and—don't spill the water, honest." The event would be far away I told him. It wasn't quite set yet but what was my story supposed to be? Now I'm into his costume shop?

But something in my brain tickled. Edward Holmberg and I had brushed shoulders in the elevator last week, right as he complimented me on my over-the-knee boots, the new stretch vinyl. He'd said something outrageous, like, was it—wouldn't it be great, to see the Nutcracker tap? His scent of English Leather had drifted my mind up and away, over the musk of the dance. Edward Holmberg was on the MDT board, a designing man at Schlamp's. Uptown's premiere women's store.

I ripped the card off the board and stuffed it in my bag, slicing my other hand. Mr. Bourman and I were still on the same wave, and I wanted to keep it that way. Onto the elevator I went, to the refuge of the tap studio, leaving all those ballet dancers and their fabulous collarbones behind. An entire land of Audrey Hepburns.

The buzz, however, was it ever out. My children, my tap students, somersaulted across the tap studio floor, squeaking like mice, pausing on their backs to wiggle hands and feet in the air, just like in the Nutcracker. I had two minutes until class-time.

I flew down the hallway to the costume department. "What's about the Tapping Nutcracker?" I waved the invitation. Oh, my gosh, I knew the look on their faces. They knew nothing. I saw that look last May when I suggested to a room full of ballet dancers that tap dancers could open the arts center.

I clicked back into the hallway, snapping my leotard down in back with a loose finger, hitching my dance bag on the opposite shoulder, back to my tap den.

Big!

Edward Holmberg leaned on my piano. Something was afoot. I'd only glimpsed him that once since the night of the Big Tap. He'd partnered Loyce down Hennepin Avenue, center front row with me, in his red blazer. Now his black-plum suit draped elegantly. His blond hair was not ruffled. Edward had a silver invitation in his hand.

"Wouldn't it be—interesting—to see the tappers in Nutcracker costumes?" he asked. I sloughed a cloud of rosin powder up from the floor as I went. It must have clogged my head.

Because as much as I idolized those costumes and dancers, I had no answer whatsoever. Lynn the registrar was no help. He stood in the far corner of the studio, checking children against the names on his clipboard. Every mouse was lined at the barre now, expectant, so I heard Edward's every word: "Beth, do what you can. It's a benefit. Half will be a fashion show, but there is a stage on either end of the giant space, and you can have those all to yourself. The runway for the models connects them. Use that too."

What were my options? The invitation was out. It was three weeks away, December 3.

"Really," he said. "If you want, just do the solo yourself. Whatever you do will be perfect." And that was the last I saw Edward Holmberg until I took the stage the day of the benefit.

I did have to admit, the idea was golden. And I could have—done nothing. Or they could have played Nutcracker music at the fashion show, dubbed some taps over for the "March Militaire."

At home, Tom lowered his chin, his eyes never so far beneath his raised eyebrows. "Well, it's over in twenty-four days," he said, calculating. I dropped to the floor, sat on my heels and watched the fire in the fireplace dance. Oh. My. Gosh.

I knew the feeling, that this-could-be-a-catastrophe heat in my head.

But it was a fantasy, no doubt. I'd never even imagined it could happen, the tappers in the ballet costumes, those million-dollar creations. The ballet dancers were busy with production, after all. This was an opportunity. I could just choreograph and dance the *Nutcracker*?

But. My tappers. I had some nice ones, and they'd just hoofed down the avenue with everyone who could find tap shoes—or paint their feet silver. Yes, it had been a great way for all the tappers in Hennepin County to kick off fall. We'd welcomed everyone into our ranks. But now I could give my tappers another kind of challenge.

Done.

I'd have soldiers, snowflakes, and mice in my Nutcracker. And it wasn't as though we'd be stranded. We'd be alongside a fashion show, alternating.

But I'd wasted a night of classes that could have been rehearsal time. With next Thursday Thanksgiving, I only had two nights of classes, and two noon hours. And tappers had day jobs. I rubbed my thumb on the fuzzy Nutcracker on the invitation so long his tummy went bare.

I'd gotten from minus zero to full production in forty-five seconds.

Anyway, the next noon I noticed: a new invitation went up on the MDT board and it stayed right there, tacked to the wall. I'm doing it: the invitation said.

Two days later, Margaret Morris at the *Star* sent a photographer. I thought of the day Loyce Houlton, artistic director, had roared to the phone. An article had run, and it said she was organizing the tap dancers. In fact she didn't know about the tap opening. She had her own concert season opener that week, a new building, studios, board, PR woman, school director and 1,000 students registered. Besides her performing company. "I have a tap teacher," she said to the person at the paper. "Come photograph her! She's the organizer," Loyce had said, by then in a purr. I did not expect to have my picture taken any time soon.

And now I had a note: Darlene Pfister would be that *Star* photographer. I should come early for my class on Friday for the photo.

The costume shop fit me pronto that day. The photo, done minutes later.

That night Margaret Morris The Columnist called me at home. The soldiers would be a cappella, I told her, a rhythmic wonder of a dance. The snowflakes—I had my childhood 78 rpm, "Let it Snow." My dance would be the Nutcracker track, the "Miniature Overture." Someone had told her we'd have twelve soldiers, same of snowflakes, and three mice. Maybe that's how many costumes they'd spare. But I could meet that. I thought the Minnesota Dance Theatre had a rule: we could land on our feet when dropped from the ceiling.

But how could we go wrong? The runway would keep the soldiers in a straight row.

The snowflakes would flit stage to stage on the runway, and the mice would somersault and tap the runway, in the antics of the ballet mice. I'd end the show, the Nutcracker, turn the length of the catwalk, dance on either stage.

If I could rehearse on it. Criminy.

If we had not already had the soldier routine rehearsed, a blessing from Jenney Franco, who showed it to me after a class, then taught it, I would have been one more step past panic. She had learned it from her tap teacher growing up, who was seventy-two now. I thought seventy-two was really really old then. We had history.

Five days out, a message came from Edward Holmberg: so many tickets had been sold that I'd lost one of the performing stages to seating.

I rechoreographed, on our last class before the show. But could we rehearse on the runway? I chased down John Linnerson, the man who knew all at the Minnesota Dance Theatre. He could build anything, a mousetrap, or a cannon that fired. John could solve anything.

"Beth, just have the dancers come first thing in the morning. As soon as the runway goes up, they can test it." John Linnerson never looked flustered, never questioned if something could work, just worked it out.

The day before the show my photo danced in the paper, more of a story than I'd ever expected. The costume was beautiful. It had all happened so fast. To me it looked like I'd dropped from the sky in the Nutcracker suit.

Steve Adelman and Sharon Anderson, *Twin Cities Today*—who did the helicopter coverage that cinched the Big Tap into the *Guinness World Book*—were in Margaret's column as well. They were getting married at Lutsen, up north. At least I wasn't planning a wedding.

That night I went to the dance theatre to rehearse myself. At the end of the hall, outside my studio, a rack glowed, twelve red-velvet and gold soldier costumes. And another rack of fluff sparkled beyond that—eight white tulle snowflake skirts. Enormous crates stacked, held the towering soldier hats and plumes, three mouse heads and their foam tummies.

Just when I was smiling at the thought of Kristin, Vanessa, and little Anne Marie in foam tummies, I sobered. Inside, on the piano, the

Nutcracker mask was stern. A note by its side made me pause: "Snowflake costumes sheer. Band-aid all nipples."

And I was just getting the Christmas spirit. I'd even forgotten that mere bodies were in those snowflake suits. Or that the Nutcracker wore a mask. And a sword. I wondered if someone somewhere had a runway. I needed to spin down it, just to see.

I snapped into the soldier jacket, donned the hat. Some moments in time are indelible.

That's me I saw turning in the mirror, saluting and clicking. I had only ever seen Mark Townes dance this costume, at Northrop Auditorium—seats 5,000, and me. I sat in the highest row. Was this a dream? I took the head off to be sure it was me. I was certain I was the only teacher at the dance theatre to have worn this costume. Was I the only dancer in a studio this late as well? I slid my fingers up and down my sleeves, over the braid. It stretched with me. I worked far into the night. I still hadn't tried the runway. I tried not to sweat.

Although I needn't have worried. The dance theatre costume shop had me collect money for dry cleaning from each dancer—each one who danced this benefit for Nutcracker costumes. Fortunately the tappers hadn't given up their day jobs, not yet.

Gayle Peterson and Annie Scheumbauer salute in the studio. (Courtesy of Deanna Carlson)

The next day, just before we went on, Beverly Semon, MDT's general manager, came to our holding room to marvel at the tappers in their costumes. The dancers turned for each other, stroked each others' hats. They pressed their stick-on red circle cheeks in place and grinned like they'd just flossed their teeth. It's time, Bev said.

The snowflakes pulled thick white socks over their tap shoes, so they wouldn't make noise on the metal stairs or backstage. They lined up behind the curtain for the start, pitching socks into a bucket.

BIG!

My blue seventy-eight record started with a scratch, and off they floated, clicking over the stage. The mice tumbled down the runway, gauging the edge through their huge mouse heads, all the while peering over their foam tummies. Smooth, everything was smooth.

But it was live entertainment and there were out-takes. The a cappella taps pounded the floor, faster, louder, rhythms more and more complex. Because the dancers were already glancing warily at the runway edge, they did see the widening cracks. What no one could predict was that my row of a dozen soldiers tap-vibrated the runway sections apart, like the fashion models never could.

They looked like marionettes, beating dark lashes down and up—because they couldn't risk tipping their heads long to look. Their hats were heavy and enormous, could topple.

The sections of the runway literally bounced in time, moving ever apart. Technicians flew under the sides of the runway. They desperately held the sections together.

I didn't believe anyone in that audience even knew. I only patched the story together by talking to different people. For my part, I had never spun down a runway and back either, but I did. I'd left the heavy mask with the small eye holes in the studio. It fooled around with my balance. I had new respect for dancers in masks.

As for the tappers—if they hadn't already had their day on Hennepin, they had it now, in million-dollar costumes, on a stage of their own—sheer joy. I would list their names but we weren't on the program. The Tapping Nutcracker program was printed before I said, "Yes." A wildly successful event.

Model on runway. (Philip Prowse. Courtesy of Minnesota Dance Theatre)

Scenes from the *Nutcracker*. (Philip Prowse. Courtesy of Minnesota Dance Theatre)

2

At the Governor's Mansion On Christmas Eve

Gretchen Quie, the governor's wife, invited me to do the Nutcracker tap dance for a television special. The governor's residence. In their solarium. On Christmas Eve. Some things even I could hardly imagine. The Nutcracker was a celebrity bar none, to me.

So Tom and Mark and Kristin and I got in the car—me in my red velvet Nutcracker suit. It wasn't really mine; I just said it was. It seemed as though it was by then.

My family laughed as we went, watching the people we passed—me in the front seat, red vinyl circles stuck to my cheeks, my plumed hat sitting high on my lap. All I could do was wave, all the while keeping my taps out of the slush on the car mat.

But I was not out of place. My kids were cool about what I did. I knew because once I found myself in their Blake School mascot costume, a bear, tap dancing. Long story. I'd been on a committee where it was decided we needed to get the students' attention at their Monday convocation. Stir up spirit for their annual school carnival.

I'd waited backstage to go on, talking to a woman. But in a flurry, she'd handed her notes to the school director, saying: "My Charlie would be so embarrassed if his mother stepped out and made an announcement." Her voice dwindled when she caught that I was Mark and Kristin's mother, me, in my tap shoes, a big furry suit, a giant bear head.

On stage I went. I searched the crowd for Mark and Kristin, as best I could through tiny eye holes in the heavy head. They were laughing, elbowing with their friends, just fine.

So that night I entered the governor's mansion with my children. They sat cross-legged by the wall. Scrooge from the Guthrie Theater passed. He'd scene with Marley in the living room. My marble floor in the solarium reflected like a mirror. I couldn't risk falling. I shook rosin on it, coated it with the tacky yellow-powder. The powder coated the furniture legs. I couldn't come or go from the room again because I'd track. But I wouldn't fall.

I was entertained, especially by a beautiful young woman in a flowing white nightgown, twelve lighted candles in a wreath balanced on her head. She climbed the stairs to a bedroom where they said she'd lie in bed, propped on pillows, to sing a Scandinavian traditional holiday song.

What if she nodded like a Lennon sister while she sang? I wondered about dripping candle wax while I waited. (After, I learned that it was her mother, Carolyn Lenner, who was in the bed. Her daughter with the candles, Sarah Quie—married to the governor's son, Joel—was playing the part of St. Lucia, would sing to her. The candles symbolized light in winter's darkness and the fire that could not consume St. Lucia.)

Tom stayed in the entry, talking to the producer. His laugh reached me. Later I learned the producer asked Tom if I were his daughter. Not outrageous because not many mothers of pre-teens came tap-dancing to the governor's house. I loved Tom's laugh.

I did my dance, gripping the slippery marble floor with the rubber pads on the balls of my tap shoes, confident that if I fell, they'd edit. I didn't fall and I went full out, spinning the end.

I didn't see the show because we were at Christmas with my family, home where I grew up, in Mason City, Iowa, home of *The Music Man*.

But I had my eye on another what if?

What if we did a marching band, blocks long, like the 1,801 tap dancers?

3

Garrison Keillor: A Prairie Home Companion New Year's Eve

I ended up playing Stump the Taps with Garrison Keillor on *Prairie Home Companion*, on New Year's Eve. It came about because I'd noticed that 1930s film star Eleanor Powell had tap-danced on radio. I'd written to her to ask how that went.

She'd said that the show staff had not thought about a tap dancer and the floor—and when she got to the studio, it was carpeted. And so they took a door off its hinges and she tapped on the door!

I relayed the story to Garrison, in a letter. He might like tap dancing. Soon I opened a letter from his producer, Margaret Moos. She said, in part:

> We would love to have you join us for a live broadcast . . . would New Year's Eve be a possibility for you? . . . Our thought would be to have you dance to the Butch Thompson Trio, our house band . . . If this sounds interesting to you . . . We do have a piece of plywood handy, so we won't have to unhinge a door . . .

Maybe I tapped around the lake, I was that excited. I was in such a shuffle on that path that day that when I passed a smiling Bobby McFerrin—

the Don't Worry, Be Happy Bobby—who by then was conducting the St. Paul Chamber Orchestra, I was certain I had a connection! I offered to teach him tap, on the dock. The man and his rhythms. I was on a roll.

Interesting as the proposal was, as much as he lingered, he had projects higher on his list and suspected to tap dance well would be quite an investment. (Not a "no," though, and, after that, I clattered every time we crossed paths.)

But I had Butch Thompson and the old wood floor of the World Theatre coming soon. (Now the World is the Fitzgerald Theatre, named after St. Paul's Scott Fitzgerald, a change spear-headed by Garrison.) I had only days to go until the show.

And then I waltzed in my front door to this: to egg me on, I swear, the voice of Noah Adams floated on MPR, his voice sure: "If I had to pick only one pianist and be like him/her, or hear only one, it would be just Butch Thompson, his blues and stride and jazz, touches of Joplin and Jelly Roll Morton, Eubie Blake." I was waiting for something as big as Christmas.

At the rehearsal, day before the performance, Garrison asked what music I wanted for accompaniment. I said—"anything Butch Thompson plays on the piano will be perfect." The first thing he played, "Blue Skies," was perfect.

But then Garrison, being Garrison, surprised us live on the show, and played "Stump the Taps." He requested Butch play "Amazing Grace."

Being Catholic, I didn't realize—in the moment—that "Amazing Grace" was a hymn. It was not played in my church anyway, at least not by the 1980s. Anyway, it was just out of context. But as Butch played, it did seem to have a pondering mood, so I jumped right in, graceful as I could. It was radio, after all. Hopefully I was appropriate. It was Garrison's idea and he was funny. By the time we got to the "Minnesota Rouser" and "Claire de Lune," I was on. For the finale, Tom rigged Christmas tree lights up the side seams of my trousers, for the final spins. Hours after I would attend seven park parties before midnight and collect folks to do a Dancing One-Hundred routine—in the shape of the number one-hundred—along the river to celebrate the 100th Birthday of the Park Board. At midnight, at New Years Eve on the River, I'd direct the crowd in a Minnesota dance that featured kicking ice off tires, catching snowflakes with tongues and slapping mittens, to Tom Bernett's "The Minneapple."

Beth and Park Director Lawrence Hutera, later, New Year's Eve.

Just as a rule of thumb—and the people were so much fun—but don't try to teach a dance on New Year's Eve.

But back to the darkened stage of the World Theatre, Garrison observed: "And there she goes, in her lighted pants, spinning to the last rousing chorus."

I also danced to the opening theme, the "Powdermilk Biscuit" song, which is actually a traditional blue-grass tune, "Roll in My Sweet Baby's Arms." And I did a skit with Garrison and Prudence Johnson, Mood Shoes, a story about a man with retractable taps, wheels and blades, all inside his shoes. Also performing on that night was Emily Kagan, the national looncalling champion.

A surprise: the musicians invited Sonny Lyon, an ex-vaudevillian at the dance theatre—a tap dancer and pianist—to be backstage. He looked tiny against the back walls behind the curtain. Old theaters were many-storied and raw. One never got used to the world above the stage with all the pulleys. A little town of technicians could run back and forth on the narrow boards. I felt part of the long-past era of the theatre with Sonny and Red the drummer telling their history. Sonny's sisters, Irma and Genevieve, even danced with

Beth in lighted pants. (Courtesy of Minda Associates)

Bill Robinson when he came to the El Lago Theatre in 1932. And here I was, tied in.

I was most privileged to talk to him it turned out, because dear Sonny lost his voice to throat cancer not that much later, and the tales ended. He still enjoyed stopping by our house to pick up Kristin to take her to music events because she didn't ever stop talking, not with a listener like Sonny. And when I'd talk to him on the phone, I would close my eyes and hang loose because some of his words were understandable, through his implanted throat microphone. Off we'd go, patching our memories together. He gave me the pictures. Towards the end of his life he gave us his cane, a pencil-thin, gold-tipped one, only two and a half feet tall, from our little Sonny.

That evening, during the show, I stood by Garrison, awaiting my stage entrance. I stayed quiet because his live monologues were improvised, and I thought he wanted to concentrate. However, Garrison leaned on the ropes of the curtain. He eyed my large poppy-colored bag, large enough to keep a piano in. "You will never be struck by a car," he said. I never got jokes right away but for some reason I got him. (He thought the red bag would work better than a stoplight in an intersection.)

I told him I loved being there. Silence.

I told him he was taller than I thought. Nothing.

Since I was almost six feet tall and staring into his collar, his height did seem worth a comment.

"The audience looks like chickens," I said. I'd always thought that but never shared it. From the stage their heads pecked back and forth, from program to stage, perhaps with an aside to their seat-mate.

So off we went, chatting, me and Garrison Keillor. I thrived in the wonder of it all. Because I'd learned that if you say one thing to Garrison Keillor that is postured or contrived or even just polite, you'd have no companion at all.

We talked up until the second he abruptly bailed and walked onstage, no notes, and delivered a twenty-minute monologue. I stood in awe at his honesty and sense of self. I wondered what being a teen was like for him. Maybe like it was for me, just cruising through peers, tap dancing our song.

That night, in Mason City, Iowa, my father taped the show on two cassette tapes. My mother only had one thing to say. She thought Mr. Keillor's stories got a bit windy. My dad labeled the tape and mailed it to me. He was pleased that when the first cassette ran out, he only lost a few seconds, which was good because I was next.

Later, I asked Garrison to write a library cheer for a book festival that I directed in 1989. He had one ready.

At the opening of the Minnesota Festival of the Book in Rice Park, St. Paul, the mood was uproarious. The keynote speaker was not. Imagine Garrison's voice. It came and went like this:

> Where do you go for the poetry? L-I-B-R-A-R-Y!
> I said where do you go for history? L-I-B-R-A-R-Y!
> When I say Library: You say Card.
> Library! Card! Library! Card!
> I got one today and it wasn't too hard
> Library! Card! Library! Card!
> Yes. Yes. Yes. Yes.

Even with just this phrase or two, even ten percent of Garrison is a very big deal. The entire cheer is still on the website of the Friends of the St. Paul Public Library—http://bit.ly/n2RbVU.

On another occasion, Garrison was very serious. He called me on the phone, out of nowhere. He'd read a newspaper article that said a large event would take place. It said it would set a world record. "And to be sure, Guinness book expert Beth Obermeyer is working on the project." I checked another paper, a columnist in *Skyway News*: "Our Twin City Guinness authority, Beth Obermeyer, will aid . . . more than likely a world's record."

No way was the event going to break any record. I knew it because I knew there was no record in the book for this. And now I knew Garrison knew it. I was hired to add some color to the event, but, of course, when one sentence in the news release said it might be a world record and the next sentence: "Beth Obermeyer, who placed Twin Cities world records in the Guinness Book, is . . ." The two sentences that close together caused confusion, intended or no.

Garrison drawled on the phone. He said he didn't like the sound of this. I was giving away all I had, my reputation. "Retreat!" he said.

But, of course, it was too late. Today the event would probably make the Guinness book because it was huge—but it was one of those events with a qualifier on it that Guinness didn't take at the time. Like the largest group of tap dancers by the Washington Monument. It had to be flat out the largest group of tap dancers. There would be no several kinds of world records in tap or anything else in the book, not at that time.

And the event tuned out to be huge, great fun. But not a world record, not at all.

I am still amazed he would take time to call. I appreciated his stand at any rate. Garrison helped me realize not to be muddy. I couldn't blame anyone but me. I was the boss of myself.

I analyzed my next world record, imagined it. I did not want to screw it up.

At any rate, Garrison is in my book. And I am thrilled to be mentioned in his: *A Prairie Home Commonplace Book: 25 Years on the Air with Garrison Keillor.*

His radio show, from which he will retire at age seventy (we are the exact same age) has 600 stations and reaches four million people. He truly holds onto himself through it all. I loved being nearby, to feel that kind of straight-forward energy.

I still think he should have a tap dancer in his All Star Shoe Band.

4

With Christopher Plummer: The British Series, Minnesota Orchestra

The beat went on.

Next was *The Boy Friend* with the Minnesota Orchestra. I knew there was a tap solo in the score somewhere, and I called. Three times. Someone had to do it, and as long as they didn't know who yet—I could do this.

Finally the call came. I'd do a tap solo, at the moment prescribed in the score. It was the second concert of the orchestra's subscription season.

At rehearsal I awaited my point in the music. I eyed the apron of the stage where I would dance. When I did *The Tap Concerto* I had much more room but this was a much smaller part, just a pass across the stage.

But all was not that simple. The score was a suite, and it repeated itself, looped back on itself and had many variations. This was the first rehearsal, but I knew from experience with the orchestra, it was the only rehearsal. The point was to get it right: one run-through.

And so, to be foolproof, and I felt like a dummy—I listened to my cassette tape at home—and timed my entrance point from the start of my part, "Polly's Dream," a free fantasy on tunes from the score. I mean I literally counted the seconds to my part. I did read and understand music. But what if my mind wandered while standing behind the curtain? Surely no one would notice. I hid my huge white-plastic teaching watch with the big numbers and the sweep-second hand under my sequin sleeve.

I waited. The movements of music passed by. I gripped the curtain, ready to launch on one-thirty-second of a count.

And the moment arrived. But the conductor, Sir Neville Marriner, dropped his arms. "Take a break, back in twenty." A dollup of pent-up energy dropped to my toenails. I turned.

Standing behind my black lycra-leotarded butt had been Christopher Plummer. How long I don't know. So what I saw when I turned was the captain in the *Sound of Music*. Would that make me Julie Andrews?

I lost it. He'd been listed for the concert for the first time only that morning, and I'd missed it. After intermission, he'd do a narration from *Henry V*, to incidental music by Walton.

So in my head—his T-shirt and jeans turned green, a wool military uniform—in my head. My eyes burned from staying open. What I finally said was unquotable. But it was fine. Because as the week went by—we did the show several times—I found he was not a sentimental man. I read now that at the time of filming he referred to the "Sound of Mucus." Julie Andrews was "like a life-long valentine." But by the time I met him, if he really said that, he was definitely mellow and quite fond of *Sound of Music* and its place in history. To be fair, he has played most of the great roles in classic repertoire.

"I guess we're the soloists tonight," is what he said.

Would I like to go to dinner after the performance, across the street from the hall, with Neville Marriner and all of our partners, six of us in all? Oh. Yes. I would.

I retreated immediately to the Green Room, talked with musicians, and tried to reserve the front of my brain for the dance I was about to rehearse.

And the rehearsal did go well, I think. So well that Sir Neville Marriner said, from his podium: "Beth, can you add one more solo, measures 78 to 110?" Or something.

Big!

Henry Charles Smith slowly pulled to his feet, in the empty auditorium. He was the conductor when I did the *Tap Concerto* with the orchestra. Could it be he was there in case the tap dancer got mixed up? But I was okay. It certainly gave me something to do in the hours between rehearsal and performance.

After the rehearsal with the orchestra, I walked six blocks down Hennepin to MDT, costume over my arm, to do my own quick dress rehearsal.

But as I spun in front of the studio mirror, I was mortified. My white knit underpants—dance pants yes, got them at Mr. Teener's—they should have been perfect—but under a cream-colored dress, as I turned, they glowed. I looked like, read like—I was dancing in my underwear.

And I'd really rather not relive that part of grade school when I spent my mornings in the church basement rehearsing the school operetta or the town's "Varieties"—the whole town was in it—when I whirled my dance and my underpants showed.

So at home, two hours before curtain call, I dipped my iridescent-in-my-mind dance pants into a cup of hot tea, lifting with a fork every half minute to see the color. I doubted Mr. Teener delivered. If I screwed that up—

Adding a minute because wet fabric is always a darker shade than dry, I hung the pants on a cupboard handle. And absentmindedly—I drank my tea!

As my underwear dripped onto the counter and beyond, I punched "The Boy Friend" tape cassette back and forth, patiently counting measures to number 78, listening to my new music, pattering away barefoot on the cold quarry tile. Thirty-nine times over and over.

That evening I went to Orchestra Hall early and found my dressing room with a star and my name, right next to the door with a star and "Christopher Plummer." This was getting absurdly spectacular. But this kind of thing always seemed normal in the moment.

I stepped into my room and eyed my costume, the dress with silk panels for a skirt, ones that let a leg show through. The sparkles I sewed on the top caught every light.

And now, in my dressing room with the star on it, next to a room with a star for Christopher Plummer, my underpants the right shade for my dress, I spun the skirt panels out. I was satisfied.

Rehearsing at this point would do no good, so I stepped back out the door. I gave my camera to Henry Charles Smith. I asked him to take my photo with Mr. Plummer.

And he did. I got a photo with Mr. Plummer and then Christopher took one of me with Mr. Smith. And Mr. Smith took a photo of me with my neighbor, Kensley Rosen, the tall and elegant violinist in the orchestra. I hoped that was okay. Usually there is a photographer to get the photo when a celebrity is about.

At any rate, the performance that evening was like a trip to the moon. I sat backstage after I danced and listened to Christopher Plummer's Shakespeare voice in Act II.

After, we stood in line by the stage door and met anyone who came backstage.

One person was just for me, or it seemed that way: Barbara Flanagan, columnist at the *Star*. "Your dance wasn't very long, but I loved your taps." It was the first time we'd met, I realized. It curled my toes.

We moved across the street, the six of us, and settled to an elegant table. Christopher Plummer's wife, Elaine Taylor, said she danced the exact same tap part in *The Boy Friend*,

Christopher Plummer and Beth.

in a production in London. She talked about the theatre scene there. They assured me my solo may not have been long, but I was as good as any they'd seen in it.

My mother always said if someone gave me a really big compliment, all I had to do was say thank you. What I was thinking was that I was sort of home free. I was chosen because tap was my specialty. Someone in the theatre production of *The Boy Friend* would have to act, sing and dance, all three, and tap might not be their strongest talent.

We sat and the evening went on for hours. Tom was the one who caught Mr. Plummer's interest because Christopher served as architect on five home remodels for himself and Elaine, two in Connecticut, one in London, one in France, one in Hollywood. They spoke of Philip Johnson, the architect who designed the IDS Center in Minneapolis, the AT&T building in New York and Johnson's own glass home in Connecticut, near Plummer's. I was proud of Tom, a star of the dinner. He deserved it.

The restaurant closed, technically, but the staff lined the window wall, their hands behind their backs, at attention. Tom and I felt like we knew him by this time and it could be difficult to get through the layer of seven Tony Award nominations and 100 feature films.

And then Christopher showed us a trick. He lighted a paper that wrapped our Italian dessert and it floated to the ceiling and hovered. He lit all our papers unless we wanted to try it.

We were out of control, and how wonderful it was after a great night of dancing and music and theatre.

Now he has written a memoir, *In Spite of Myself*, interesting because of its history of theatre. But I think the Christopher Plummer with Elaine, the relaxed view we got of him that night—that was the Christopher to know about.

My parents listened to the live broadcast, and my father taped it for me. My mother was curious about how, after the end of the show, the narrator described every bow, every move we made, what I was wearing. She loved that. If I had ever noticed that they did this at the end of concerts, described the applause and bows, I didn't remember, so I had no explanation for her. My dress was from Schlamp's, the designer clothing store near me.

The next morning, the *Minneapolis Star* said I was, ". . . in the words of Mel Brooks, 'The Tops in Taps.'"

5
The Tap-Dance Concerto Tours with the Minnesota Orchestra

Throughout all of this the Minnesota Orchestra continued to do *The Tap Concerto*. I found through the years that most things happened when I took the initiative. This was no exception.

In general, I think if we wait for something to come to us—it usually doesn't happen, at least for a while. I've kept a list of all the ideas I have had over the years, for events and for dance. Perhaps half a dozen I proposed out of nowhere—out of fifty—really happened at that moment. I wanted an Easter Parade on the Nicollet Mall, just the people. I imagined a real dog and pony show for a realtor. I wanted a Kick the Can band for recycling. Kids, everyone, kicking cans.

But it didn't take long until a fair number of those inquiries did turn into performances and/or events when their time was right. I was available was what I said: here was an idea. And even though the idea I proposed might not happen in the moment, they often called later with a need or idea of their own. Somebody once told me that you have to get in the ring a lot to win a few, and I think that is true. All it took was to write a paragraph or two on a good idea and send it to a possible home.

The *Tap Concerto*, for one, came about when I headed just one block over to visit with my neighbor—who would be my neighbor for decades more—Kensley Rosen, a violinist with the Minnesota Orchestra. His house was by the bus stop, and so on that day I went early and asked. Had he ever heard of the *Tap Concerto*? His two dogs weren't interested, but Kensley had an answer.

Call Henry Charles Smith, conductor at the orchestra, he said. He'd speak of it with "Henry" first.

I did. Mr. Smith said he'd get me the cassette tape and the score and if I wanted, to give it a try. I should work out the first movement. Let him know when. He'd take a look.

Did I ever take a look. The concerto was twenty minutes long, in four movements: Toccata, Pantomime, Minuet, and Rondo. It filled me, grounded me: I grew up in ballet as well as tap, played classical piano.

Kensley Rosen, violinist for the Minnesota Orchestra. (Henry Charles Smith)

When I got the opportunity to do something that was scored this beautifully, for a tap dancer, the desire to work it out came easy. What would have been hard: having to do something I hated that was not well conceived by the time I got it.

Beth, age twenty, in Gounod's *Ave Maria*, 1963. (Don Gerdes, Iowa State University, journalism)

A year later I showed him the first movement. He sat alone in the huge hall. I wound my way up the side stairs to the stage and behind the curtain to come out to face him. This was the first time I tapped on the apron of the stage of Orchestra Hall. I had the sound tape he'd given me for accompaniment. I tapped the first movement: "Toccata."

"Keep going," he'd said. The two words an artist loves to hear.

Months later, after my performance of the piece, a drummer in the orchestra tapped his finger on the score. How had I figured it out, my line of percussion? A drummer's part on a score is all on one line, the note of C. The rhythm the only direction—half notes, quarter notes, and so on.

A dancer couldn't do the *Tap Concerto* without reading music, or shouldn't. I showed him my attack. I wrote the count over the measures as we do in tap, +8 +a1, A+a2. That's another way to remember the rhythm while I visualize the steps (and then the body). I would scat it, then write it down. I was part of the music, on the score.

I had this same conversation with a ballet dancer, I told him. She shrugged off that I counted measures 1 to 8 in 4/4 time, instead of 1-4. It's what tappers do. It's just a convenient block to play with when producing audible complex rhythms.

But I always notice tap dancers have no trouble staying in unison if the rhythm is prescribed (not improvisational). Ballet photos often show the dancers just one-sixty-fourth of a count off or even half a count off. They don't have the sound guide a tap dancer does. To be fair, they may be stretching into very specific lines, whereas a tapper wants to make a sound on a count.

The drummer circled measures on the music. He said I ranged a bit away from the score at rehearsal. I did hear a "No" once, behind me. But I did have some leeway with the rhythms in the *Tap Concerto*, I told him, because composer Morton Gould was not a tap dancer. Some rhythms did not translate well to feet; a slight adjustment mattered little. But good to know his take.

And it wasn't a problem because the bigger fact was that Mr. Gould came up with patterns I never would have, so even if I only came close in places, it still would be unique. Sometimes he had the tap dancer pause completely for measures at a time, during a movement of the music, like any instrument might do.

Later, Morton Gould wrote me a letter and said I interpreted it well, stayed with his intentions, did not go too far. I had a "serious sensitivity to the work and its possibilities." He lamented in the letter that at least one named dancer who had performed the piece with a major orchestra had "got too far away from the integrated rhythmic patterns I indicated between soloist and orchestra. And I feel his liberties lessened the impact of the work."

I thrived on the beauty of those Morton Gould rhythms. I knew, because of an injury, I was down on back flexibility, but I could make up for it in rhythms. Decades later I watched Jennifer Gray on *Dancing with the Stars* make up for a neck left stiff from cancer surgery, and I knew my challenge was small.

I did want to think Morton Gould's favorite tap soloist in his *Tap Concerto* may have been my childhood teacher in Mason City, Iowa, Dean Diggins. Mr. Gould visited Dean's barn/studio/gallery in Maine when Dean choreographed the piece. (But I didn't know that at the time. When we re-connected (google Dean Diggins) we found not only had we both done the concerto, we'd also both done tapping Nutcrackers.)

Conductor Henry Charles Smith did write to me after: "Thank you so much for your wonderful performances with our orchestra. You are very creative and exciting as an artist. It was fun for me to be doing something that has never been done before in our part of the country."

Performing the *Tap Concerto* with the orchestra was the solo experience of a lifetime.

Beth at a *Tap Concerto* rehearsal. (Courtesy of David Beckman)

6

Paul Draper, the Tap-Dancer's Tap-Dancer

Frank Bourman, director, School of the Minnesota Dance Theatre, still had tap dancers on his mind, in a good way. He arranged a tap seminar—at the dance theatre, for the summer after the Big Tap.

Paul Draper would come to us, so important a dancer that we all ended up on Charles Kuralt's television show. Having Paul Draper at MDT for two weeks would be like having a famous impresario come teach piano if I were director of the music department at the University of Minnesota. Mr. Bourman and I were in agreement on this one and I appreciated that he did this for the tap dancers. He did, after all, survive the 1,801 tap dancers opening his arts center.

Who was Paul Draper? When I say he was a tap dancer's tap dancer it is because he did things most tap dancers hadn't even thought of and didn't know existed.

Example: everyone knows what a wing looks like, in tap dance. A wing, to many, is when the arms windmill and the legs shoot out to the sides, simultaneously, over and over, fireworks. But to Paul Draper a wing was the footwork only, minus the arms and the fanfare. Most tap dancers ignore this, but a wing is an impossible brush out to the side and back with one foot while the other foot tucks back, no weight. Paul's face could sometimes betray him, strained. (On Google, just from his name, one can seen many beautiful examples of a young Paul Draper.)

Most of the students who signed up for Paul's class at MDT were area teachers. For us it was a great time to get together again, this time to learn and improve ourselves.

Paul Draper was near the end of his career when I met him. Three decades my senior, he excelled, startled us. An engineer by trade, early on he transferred his mathematical head into the rhythms of tap dancing. But the arts had been in his veins already.

His mother was Helen Vosseler, a ballerina with George Balanchine at the American Ballet Theatre. His father was a talented concert singer. His Aunt Muriel was a noted author and lecturer; another aunt, Ruth Draper, was an American dramatist, the undisputed queen of one-woman theatre in the twentieth century.

So perhaps it wasn't surprising that he merged tap, the art form, with ballet, to produce a combination of line and artistry, and added the sound, the music of his feet.

As a young man he landed a role in *Blue Skies*, but was replaced at the last minute by the emerging Fred Astaire, because Paul stammered and couldn't do spoken lines with any ease. Later he was black-listed by the House Committee on Un-American Activities. Like many others so listed, his infraction was resolved in time, but also like the others, his career came to a halt. The 1948 *The Time of Your Life*, is a good showcase of his dance.

Of course he never stopped dancing or developing. Today Dean Diggins—my dance teacher in my Iowa hometown—is a protégé of Paul. He recreated the Draper legend for history.

Little did I know, back in the days of the tap opening for the arts center, that I had that strong connection to Paul Draper. Dancers at the dance theatre asked—curious—who were your dance teachers? I'd say that I grew up in Mason City, Iowa, a hotbed of live entertainment and music. I didn't think I had another answer they would understand, no matter how in awe I was of my teachers. I was only a decade older than these dancers at MDT, but in dancer years that was a century.

I didn't even know to mention Rose Lorenz in Des Moines, who was Dean's teacher. Rose Lorenz was Cloris Leachman's teacher, too, and Cloris thanked Rose when she accepted her Emmy.

BIG!

When Paul Draper came to MDT, I got the word out. We filled two classes, beginner and intermediate, and waited.

I met Mr. Draper in Frank's office and took him down Hennepin Avenue to see Mr. Teener. Mr. T. and I told Paul as best we could how we happened to have 1,801 tappers at the opening of the arts center.

But it was the store and Mr. Teener that knocked Paul dead. He stood in the midst of every enhancement any performer could ever crave—skyscrapers of sequins and baubles and eyes and tails. As a child visiting Minneapolis, I thought Mr. Teener was the shoemaker who had elves come in at night. To me there was no other explanation.

At lunch, Paul asked me to scat the first eight measures of the *Tap Concerto*, a piece originally written for him. I did. "Wrong," he shouted, literally, so that the wait staff at the New French Café rushed to his side. Had what I scatted not been the opening measures, I might have backed off. Somewhere in the twenty-minute piece I had strayed just a titch, entitled to by the nature of the collaboration. But I was certain that at the start of the piece I was right on. I showed Paul my letter from Mr. Gould.

But it was Draper's personality to challenge. And mine to stop eating, stand my ground.

He even challenged my daughter, Kristin, eight, who sometimes came to lunch with us those weeks. Soon he had her selecting the right fork, acknowledging the appetizer plate. He'd order foods she'd never seen to show how the utensils should go. He had three daughters of his own, and he melted his approach, for a child. Kristin loved the special attention. She had watched his classes every day and knew when she had something going.

If Paul Draper were a flower he would be the only one in the world. He proceeded in the weeks that followed to fascinate all in the classes. Most left licking their wounds, tap dancers of all styles. And how could we be in his style after all; he was the only one like him and he had just arrived.

But what over-whelmed all of us about him was that he took tap so seriously and his style was a beautiful art form. We stayed with him.

He was the real thing. He did forward pullbacks; usually pullbacks are done back. Back pullbacks are a brush back with one foot, no weight on the other foot, so you travel on air—and land. A double pull back is when both feet brush in the air and land. A pull back is common and a front one

Big!

Paul, seventy-two, kicking.

should be no harder; but it had never occurred to us to do a pull-back the way he showed it.

He also did a four beats to a bar rhythm with one foot and three beats to a bar with the other, simultaneously, ridiculously difficult, so crazy I couldn't even sort out that he was doing it. He'd spent a lifetime developing this kind of thing.

Daily, in the classes, he sorted lifetime dancers from the second class and moved them to the beginning one. Once he said to the class of mostly teachers: "If you ever become serious about tap-dancing . . ." Startling.

His quotes from *Dance Magazine*:

"Tap is too often used as a form of exhibition rather than as an expression of something a dancer feels about the world and the people who live here . . ."

"Produce music not noise . . ."

"Tap is too often three choruses filled with sound, fury and arms and legs and no remote suggestion as to why . . ."

"Routines relieve one of becoming a dancer; you can avoid hard study by imitating steps. You learn tap by exercises, not steps."

On the last day I took photos of him. I sent him prints. One he sent back, of himself and Kristin—a kid in shorts and a polo shirt, one foot behind the other, smiling like she'd mastered it all. He wrote: "Your manners are just about perfect, Kristin." His face had an expression I'd never seen, not in classes, priceless, like this was what he came for. He'd forged a huge fan in Kristin, too.

Big!

I attended the Aspen Design Conference the next week with Tom, but through every event and talk, my head rattled with patterns and rhythms.

I still work on the puzzles that are Paul.

Above Paul Draper. At right Paul and Kristin. Below: Barbara Lotsberg, tappers at the barre. (Beth Obermeyer photos)

7

Gregory Hines
Dancer, Singer, Actor

To promote Gregory Hines's film, *Tap*, a public relations firm, Nemer Fieger, hired me to do Tap Day, at City Center. The call was just awesome, and I bounced right with it. This would be an *event* about *tap-dancing*, my two things together. Gregory himself was coming and Tri Star Pictures wanted to do the world's largest tap dance, something he would do in three other cities around the country.

The problem: we already held the record. We needed to do something else. But he also wanted a competition to pick the best solo tap dancer out of a Top Ten. Since we would be auditioning tappers every five minutes for days—I suggested putting a different dancer on the stage every five minutes for the hours leading up to the big contest at City Center.

I was also to teach the crowd a routine by Henry Le Tang, a well-known film choreographer, and Gregory's teacher in his childhood. I asked three teachers to teach it with me, one angled each direction on the stage, for the huge city center crowd. The producers provided strap-on taps for everyone. They were three-inch-wide red or green elastics with taps, grommets, and Velcro closures. Who had ever seen such a thing? Now I take them on trips because I hate to be away from my tap shoes. (I have a roll-up piano, too.)

Beth Obermeyer head to head with Gregory Hines. (From video, courtesy of Dennis Gossweiler)

The crowds at City Center lined the balconies from early on, and the sound of so many tap shoes indoors clattered against all the hard surfaces. Tapping with a crowd that dances on three levels of balconies was really really fun, by the way!

I didn't see Gregory Hines that day until the crowd did, although we'd exchanged letters in the previous two weeks. He came through the door to the arena, a guard on each side, all the same size. Gregory Hines had a magnificent body, muscular and tall.

He took time to appraise each balcony, acknowledging them with a wave to waves of cheers and screams. He didn't get hyper at all. He seemed to have walked into our living room. It was his look of appreciation that made one pause.

He stepped up onto the stage and bowed to talk to people around the edge. But what happened next took my breath away. When he moved onto the backstage area, he grasped my hands and put a kiss on each of my cheeks. By holding my hands, he kept me in place, like nothing was happening. It seemed as though something was left on each cheek, like somehow he'd really come off a movie screen. I can still feel it.

Then he ran his finger under his lapel to show he was wearing the tap stick pin I'd given him. I'd sent it in a letter he'd been given the night before. His calmness, his way of being in the moment with me—startled me because I was in the logistics of the moment, with so many dancers and judges.

The pin flashed the lights, the footprint of a tap shoe on his lapel. It was one of those moments that seemed to last forever, so much to take in and absorb.

And I would see him with the pin in many photos after that, over the years. He moved it from jacket to jacket. He must have had it gold-plated again because the gold wore off mine.

But the moment wasn't over. I did get a photo of Gregory and me in the next moments. We were on a four-hour video of the day, a small detail in a larger scene, our foreheads touching, trying to hear each other over the

Teaching the Strap-on Taps Dance. Beth is with Char Weiss, Barbara Lotsberg, Marcia Galle, and the crowd in City Center. (Jil Hopland; courtesy of Nemer Fieger)

Above: Gregory Hines engulfed in the crowd. (Jil Hopland; courtesy of Nemer Fieger) At right: Eleanor Powell's tap shoe pendant and Gregory Hines's lapel stick pin. (Beth Obermeyer)

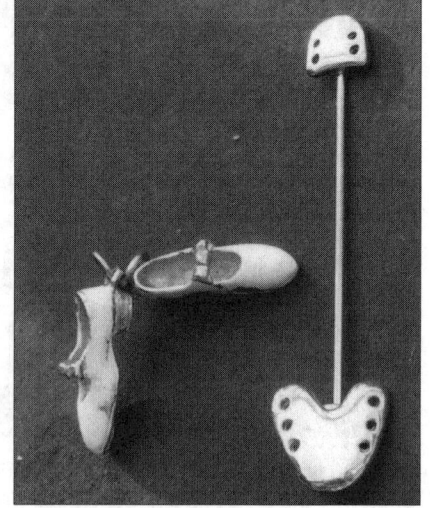

crowd; we were mostly blocked from the crowd by a banner. It was a short thrill of a lifetime to play with rhythms with Gregory Hines.

He liked to do a tap challenge—one does something, the other back. I showed him a favorite, where my toe taps clinked on their inner side edge. He didn't have on taps but he nodded and did it back, with a twist. It forever sticks in my head—his step, mine.

I take the *clink* to the side by touching the inner toe tap edges together in the air, coming down toe-heel with the propelling foot. The *clink* does not go unnoticed. In the air, it resounds. Gregory had large toe taps (Capezio Teletones), as did I, for doing this—had to. I'm sure his version will change each time he does it. (Paul Draper preferred taps so small they were like the clips men wore on their shoes in the fifties. And he did not understand how the tiniest scratch could get on our beautiful new wood floor at the dance theatre. His taps whispered.)

My other favorite memory of the day, besides seeing ten thrilled tap soloists compete, was Herbie Burkus sitting alongside Gregory Hines to judge the tappers. Herbie was the ex-vaudevillian who tapped in the front row of the 1,801 tap dancers. The third judge was Robert Moulton, professor of theatre arts and dance at the University of Minnesota. It was important to have judges who truly were tappers and yet had no close connection to local tappers. Robert Moulton debuted at eight in Vaudeville. Myron Johnson at *Ballet of the Dolls* would have been a spectacular judge, but he didn't really tap, or it was not his specialty. We should have had him judge movement for tap. We should have.

The winner of our solo contest was one of the only children in the ten finalists and the youngest: Tyheesha Collins, nine years old. Her dance was basic but exceptionally well-done, to "I've Got Rhythm." Her adoptive mother stood proud. Tyheesha was the oldest of eight children.

No one could deny her huge amount of musicality. She stood stunned by her win, sobbed into her hands. Gregory dropped to one knee by her and soon she was back to calm and did her dance again for us. I think he had her do it again so we could see what he saw, a child perfectly taught, precise, moving in her way. Her teacher, Char Weiss, also taught the second-place winner.

Gregory developed a close tie to Tyheesha over the years, and she returned to us often, especially on National Tap Day. He cared and related to all of us, as thoroughly as he could.

But it was a contest, and nine others competed well, each shining, surviving the audition of hundreds. They were chosen to present different styles to a range of music. They included:

Therese McDonald, dancing a cappella, placed second.
Wendy Gilmer, "Varsity Drag"
Kendra Berge, thirteen, all speed and turns, to "No Business like Show Business"
Michael Ford, "Tiger Rag"
Leslie Bennett Daly, a classic, to "Just in Time"
Diane Haviland, "Who's in the Strawberry Patch with Sally?" placed third.
Kirstin Spykerman, "Fabulous Feet"
Alysia Paulson, "Bugle Call Rag"
Matthew Sidotti, "Zoot Suit"

Soon after, Gregory worked into the crowd and away.

In my basement today hangs the fifteen-by-fifteen-foot white banner that hung in City Center above us, four-foot-tall red letters: "TAP DAY." Gregory's big blue signature is affixed, and it was part of the story, reigning over us all.

The next morning Joel Thom at Nemer Fieger agency called me to say that Gregory Hines tried to ring me nine times, from a phone booth at the airport. My line was busy. Gregory Hines, who personified classical tap, the cross-over actor, Tony Award 1992 for Jelly Roll Morton. That Gregory.

I was talking to my mother, long distance. She wondered if I wished I might have tapped, soloed, in the competition. Of course, I couldn't. I'd organized it. But I told her about the bit of improvising I did with Gregory at the edge of the stage.

She asked if she could have a T-shirt from the event. My mother had never worn a T-shirt. But this was a celebrity, she said, one connected to me, and she would be proud to wear it.

The next Christmas she wore the T-shirt. This was after she had fallen on some steps and not walking a great deal. She did not come to the Hines event, and I knew after the fall she never would. I could say that all she got was a T-shirt. But it is what she wanted and we were both happy.

(Thank you to Denny Gossweiler for giving her his. I didn't have one. Denny taught Kendra Berge, in the top ten.)

8

Eleanor Powell Film Star 1935 to 1945

One of the sweetest treats to come my way started right after the big tap. I fell in love. With Eleanor Powell.

Bob DeFlores, the rare tap film historian, drew her attention to the Big Tap, 1,801 tap dancers, something she said she hadn't seen since Busby Berkeley days of film, the huge patterns made from hundreds of dancers. That started a correspondence that did not end until her death only two years later in early 1982. Although I was too young to have seen Miss Powell's period films in their time, my mother had—many times over. The costume I wore in the Big Tap was made by my mother, like Eleanor's in *Born to Dance*.

Apparently my mother never saw a costume or even a step that she forgot, even though she never took dance lessons. (She did, however, "teach the Methodist boys to dance.") But she never took violin, either, and that didn't stop her from walking three miles to town every day as a youngster to be in the school orchestra. (She was not fond of the horse and carriage because she was the youngest and had to sit in the middle.)

So for me to get to know Eleanor Powell—well that was a very big deal to my mother. And it single-handedly made all my dance projects after I met Eleanor worthwhile—to my mother. She was certain Eleanor Powell was the greatest tap dancer ever, and I did not disagree. And my mother's fixation was complicated. To like a dancer's dancing she also had to love the person, her character.

And she might not have been far off because the Eleanor Powell I grew to know was every bit the kind and lovely woman of my mother's dreams—the "Queen of Rat-a-Tap," as she was known, among her grand titles. On the other hand, my mother did not like film tap star Ann Miller for a reason I don't remember. And Ginger Rogers was "only there to make Fred Astaire look good." Perhaps she confused the film personalities of Miss Miller and Miss Rogers with the real women.

When I sent Eleanor a charm, a pair of white enamel tap shoes, she sent me a note. She'd worn them to a big event and "got lots of compliments. I just adore them." Eleanor and I wore the same style white tap shoe, not a high heel, not a low flat one, either, and the pendant was it. Edith Blue at Capezio sent me several of the little white-metal tap-shoe pendants after the Big Tap. Years later I saw Edith's name was probably Edith Bloom. But Edith Blue was such an unusual name that I remembered it.

Now I was smitten.

Further, Eleanor said our Big Tap on television "looked like one of the scenes from my film *Rosalie*, with all those people. I never knew we had that many tap dancers."

It all just escalated, the back and forth, the adoration. Soon it was official: we invited Eleanor Powell to come to Minneapolis. We would tap a salute to her, an All-Tap show. MDT mailed an audition notice to five-states-worth of tap dancers.

Her reply: "At the Academy Theatre in Los Angeles, the audience told me I was the greatest thing since canned beer! How about that! Now you topped that with a salute of which I am most grateful."

Meanwhile, she fed my Hollywood fantasy. She talked a bit about meeting with Ben Vereen who was doing a book and film on Bill Robinson, and "as I knew Bill so well, there is much I can tell him for his research."

I was star struck, just a bit.

But the next sentence she said, regrettably, no. "I'm receiving another award that night here in California. It breaks my heart not to be able to be there. What an honor—I would hug each and every dancer."

BIG!

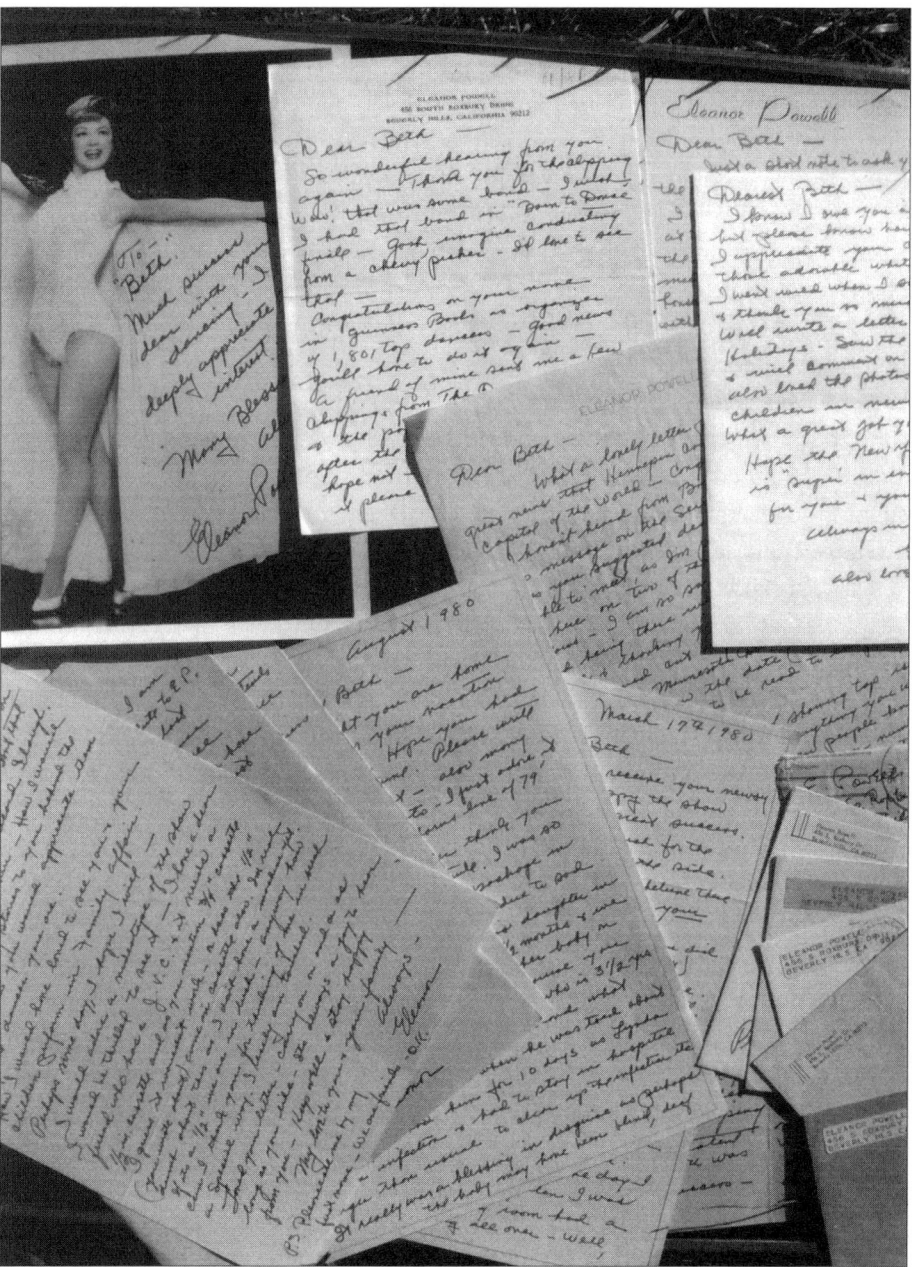

Beth's letters from Eleanor Powell. (Beth Obermeyer. Photo of Eleanor Powell courtesy of Eleanor Powell)

I think we would have been more surprised had she been able to come. And while she seemed almost too modest to be true, nothing that was ever written about her contradicted what I received in letters. Family was important to her as well. Her son Peter's birthday was the day after the tap show, and she could not be away for that.

The next February we did our all-tap show. She sent us a telegram. I sent her the video of the show and the program with notes. We chatted about our favorite book, *Jazz Dance, An American History of Vernacular Dance*, by Marshall Stern, our favorite book it turned out because it has so much tap history.

She said I should get my book on tap out, which I was writing at the time, because "there is not a good one out yet; we need one badly."

I craved knowing what an authentic step from her would be. Her suggestion was to come visit her in Los Angeles. But our winter trip was already scheduled to Florida, a business trip for Tom.

I asked for details about a tacet (tap without music) she did with Fred Astaire in a film, *Broadway Melody* of 1940. She said to pick up the tacet of the routine, "Begin the Beguine." It was their classic dance together that had been held to be the most perfect tap dance ever, the end result of their merged choreography. She said she would answer all my questions in her next letter.

It had one dancer overlapping the other, nothing difficult, just ball changes and chugs, grab offs, hops and flaps, but oh, the magnificent rhythms and interplay. When Eleanor and Fred did that tacet on film, they seemed to be amazed at the floor, like it was a third partner that somehow seeped up through their bodies. Their expressions were smug, like—who knew that floor had so much give. To see it was to start an improvisation. One needed a partner.

I noticed Fred spotted the floor a great deal when turning. Eleanor always spotted eye level. His expression was roller coaster. I never saw that look on his face when he danced with Ginger. The thrill was catching.

I sent Eleanor Powell a video of my version of her dance. She answered: "How I would love to see you perform in person; some day I hope I will." And: "Please call me by my first name, Eleanor; we are friends. Okay." "And I must compliment you on your dancing—really good!" Oh my.

BIG!

She also said: "So few people know that I choreographed all my own numbers. In fact I did a lot of the production numbers as well in my films." Her favorite floor was maple, she said, the only wood to use.

And no, it is a rumor that she collects tap routines. "I have no method of recording them. In fact I haven't a thing recorded (on records) except what I did when I sang and danced for Tommy Dorsey right after the film *Melody of '36*. I did two routines from the show on Broadway called *At Home Abroad* at Wintergarden Theatre and two from the film I'd just finished at Metro." (Metro Goldwyn Mayer, MGM.)

The next year of letters passed quickly, and we hit family highs. She hoped for a grandchild to follow her first. She didn't know yet or ever that there would be a girl, named after her. She sent a photo of herself in a period of time when she went back to performing at my age plus some.

I sent a Christmas photo of my immediate family of thirty-two that gathered at Christmas, lined up like *A Chorus Line*. We reveled in our families. She loved the photo.

A Sartor Family Christmas: A Chorus Line. Left to right: Kristin, Mark, Dommie, Julie Roth, Jean Roth, Mother; sisters Celeste Roth, Julie Beckman, and Beth Obermeyer; Father; John Roth, Tom Roth, Bob Roth, David Beckman, Tom Obermeyer, and Bob Sartor, brother.

The excitement built. "Dearest Beth," she said: "I know some day we will meet and four white tap shoes will dance up a ball. How I would love to relate many stories to you behind the scenes. I know you would appreciate them, being the dancer you are. And please . . . call me Ellie."

Sadly, a week after her appearance at a big event in Los Angeles, the Fred Astaire Salute, she was diagnosed with cancer.

That day started ominously for me. I walked the afghan hound as usual, and we smelled smoke. He skittered. Only a block from my home the Mary Tyler Moore house was aflame, the house with the third floor apartment that began each television show in her series. Painters had been burning layers of paint off the century-old house with a torch. I couldn't watch and the dog was nervous. I headed home to watch the television news. Painful. (The damage was repaired.)

Inside my door lay a letter. It was from Eleanor. The address was typed. It was a form letter. Ellie entered the hospital one day and had surgery the next, to remove a tumor on her left ovary and have a hysterectomy. She had a visiting nurse at home three days a week to give her shots. She had cancelled all future appointments for the rest of the year, under doctor's orders. "I am slowly getting stronger each day and with positive thinking I know all will go well."

But on the other side she wrote a note. "Dearest Beth. Look what happened to me, right after the Fred Astaire Tribute (April 10, 1981). I was so overwhelmed with that standing ovation, my eyes were full of tears and I almost forgot what I was going to say. I met Baryshnikov and that was a thrill. I go back to hospital July 6th for x-rays and tests and pray the shots are working to rid the ten percent of cancer. Please say a prayer, Beth. Your letter was a joy—like a ray of sunshine. Bless you, dear. So much Love, Ellie."

The letters continued. Back and forth she went, as usual, asking about me, telling me a bit about her, and always adding a funny story. She thought Miss Piggy tap-dancing with cannons behind her, as Eleanor did in *Born to Dance,* was fun. "Miss Piggy, she can do anything." "What a cherished love you are," she said, "to write such a beautiful letter."

Her name was getting shorter and shorter. Maybe it even said "E." Maybe she didn't finish writing her name. I barely got a chance to call her Ellie. I noticed how she dropped articles like "the" and said just "hospital." Her writing was clipped, lots of dashes.

Only one more letter. After chatting powerful things to me, cheerful things, she ended: "Well as for me, it's November 3rd and I've had my third chemo treatment. I go into hospital December 1st and again December 29th, four weeks to the day."

She had no way of knowing the meaning her last sentences would have. "Keep happy and keep dancing. Please thank your mother for her concern. Love as always, Eleanor Powell." My mother was pleased beyond words to be thanked by Eleanor Powell.

But I couldn't help but notice Ellie's signature. It was the full name, like she was pulling together for a formal proper end. My father called when the letter came. He was a doctor, and he saw more in it than I. The sequence of treatments was on a path, he said.

On February 11, 1982, her death at only sixty-nine years of age was reported in the papers. I sent a card and enclosed our 1,801 signatures. Barbara Flanagan announced in her column in the *Minneapolis Star*, to the tappers: the card had been sent, from all of us.

A handwritten card arrived back, from her son, Peter Ford. He said she "cherished me as a friend" and when he is in Minneapolis we will "go out a dancing, with her grandson, Aubrey." But he mourned, too.

> The passing of my mother, Eleanor Powell, was a great tragedy . . . I am her only child and we have been preparing for her passing for almost one year. But judging from the grief we feel, it was not nearly enough. She was a warm, generous, and sincere person, with time for everyone. Her talent and her heart were bountiful. We were blessed to have her in our family. There will never be another like her. My son was going to start dancing lessons with his Nana this year. She was so proud of him; there was a special love. My wife's relatives live in Wisconsin—we are going to stop in Minneapolis/St. Paul on the way up there next year. Perhaps we could introduce little Aubrey to his Nana's dancing friend. Please hold a place in your heart for a great dancer and a wonderful friend.
>
> Sincerely, Peter Ford

Her death was indeed a tragedy. She was far too young. She wanted to tell me her stories, and I wanted to write about her. I wanted to show her that I could put more of her dances on paper, too, so that they could be passed on.

But at that time, to see her dance, I had to find a theatre where a thirties or forties film was playing. I only deciphered the tacet between Eleanor and Fred because Tom brought a video machine home from his college for the weekend with a three-quarters-inch professional tape of her film. I watched the tape all night to pick it up before it all had to go back. Home video was new, only just developing.

As years passed, I was able to buy videos of her films and watch. With the advent of the Internet, I clicked up her individual routines and watched closely, one aspect at a time. I noticed that she preferred a bell-like sound from her tap, a larger tap, screwed slightly loose. So, Paul Draper liked a small tap clip fused to the shoe for a dry subtle sound, heel and toe, and Gregory Hines liked his taps big and brassy. I prefer taps like Ellie's. Liked the sound of them better as well.

Eleanor Powell had a solid ballet line, like Paul Draper, but it did not limit her. She grew up a ballet dancer, never intended to tap, even fought it.

Someone who knows no ballet can picture these steps. Entrechat-quatre, epaulment, fouette, cabriole, she could begin and end all in taps. The entrechat-quatre is the spring up, straight legs beat tight and come down like an arrow. The epaulment brings a leg up, while the body flips. A fouette turn is like a top, leg whipping in a quick circle. The cabriole: a leg up; the other smacks to it, sending it higher. Her feet were turned out in all of these ballet steps, and sometimes they stayed parallel to tap, ranging out, apart for balance.

She made the difficult look easy with her shrugs, her playfulness. Paul Draper always stayed within a ballet line, and that could bring tough compromises. He trained in ballet only as an adult.

And that does not take away from Paul Draper. He was one style—ballet placed over tap—and he did it precisely. Perhaps their differences, in part, were in their personalities.

Another aspect of her tap: her flexibility. It was the base of her lightning spins. Her center of balance was impeccable, always.

In her film, *Born to Dance*, she raised one leg straight vertical, dusted off her tap shoe. The leg raised, lowered, then she dropped into a floor-brushing back-bend.

Moments later, a lunge to the right took her into almost a split, seeming to drop through the floor as she went low. At another point, the same film, her turns were done on a two-foot-square platform; her flexibility and strength kept her absolutely on spot.

Her ability to stop from speed—turns—was startling. Her routines had composition, with the beginning and end, like any well-composed piece of music. She didn't start like a fan and run continuously as was tempting if you could, and she could. Nothing tempted her to be only flash.

She was the Mozart of tap dancing.

IN THE DECADE BEGINNING 2010, fifty-five years after her peak, I believe Eleanor Powell's fame has just started to grow. In the recent past, young tap dancers landed soundly on the side of Gregory Hines, developing the African-American style of tap, astounding rhythms, as complex as any drum, sometimes hanging over the footwork.

They'd left the jazz body line that developed in *A Chorus Line*, the jazz line over a simpler tap sound. And not followed the ballet line that Paul Draper developed to exclusivity. They'd not been into the routines taught at dance seminars. They were creating.

But with the availability of the Internet, I think the present-day wonderfully funky tappers are noticing the history of Eleanor Powell's dancing, and appreciate its complexity and ease. The new tappers are amazing in their style and have the confidence to see her as a tap-dance legend, snatch what they need, what suits them, embrace it.

And the confidence doing that takes. Gregory Hines himself once merged his style with Barishnikov, and vice versa—in *White Knights*, the film, another tap moment to keep.

9

Big Bird

I danced with Big Bird. If it had not been during school hours, Kristin would have been there.

Part of Sesame Street was based in Minneapolis, and the Ice Follies as well. One day the man (cover your eyes if you don't know this) who was inside the big yellow suit came to the dance theatre to learn—not to tap—but to *look* as though he was tap dancing. He was on ice skates in the ice version of *Sesame Street*. His name was Robin Steiner and he'd "tap" to "I Can Do That." One huge factor he'd have to overcome: ice skaters lean forward; ballet dancers are upright. I tap upright.

He needed the moves for the kind of tap I didn't usually do. What I did was show him the routine of the 1,801 tap dancers because it was designed to be viewed from a helicopter: wide side-to-side arm swings, lunging buffalos, up and down trenches.

I was almost forty years old, but I fell into the spell. *For crying out loud, Beth*, I said to myself. You're dancing with Big Bird! He might as well be Prince Charming. Because Big Bird's beauty is not just feather deep—inside the costume was a really cute guy!

10

The Doughboy

I got involved with the Pillsbury Doughboy.

At a rehearsal for the World's Largest Marching Band, I was giving directions to thousands on how the day would go. I used my arms when I talked, my "monkey arms," as my grandsons say. But everyone was laughing and I was not trying to be funny. I didn't get it. I was deep into where their bathrooms were, a dozen of them, because otherwise they'd form the world's longest line to the bathroom. Guinness really wouldn't approve. What was not funny was that I was standing high atop a drained fountain where soloists would soon stand. Something nudged me from behind, like a soft bumper car.

But I preached on, used to keeping my focus. The information I was giving out was basic, necessary but not entertaining. But they still laughed. In ripples it came. I paused between sentences. I checked to see if I was wearing pants. I ran a hand over my hair to make sure it wasn't standing straight up.

Eventually, on my shoulder, I felt a definite presence I couldn't ignore. I turned. I was eyeball to buttons with the giant Doughboy. He had been zigging and sagging behind me just out of my sight. He still mimicked me and it looked like a dance. He had every sweep of my arm, toss of my hair, and now that I'd caught him the crowd exploded with glee.

Beth with the Pillsbury Doughboy on her shoulder (Philip Prowse, courtesy of Downtown Council; Doughboy, the Pillsbury Company)

My authority for that day was gone, but it was funny.

I assume the photographer was Philip Prowse. He had done the Big Tap, the Tapping Nutcracker and all parts of the Big Band event. When I called to verify, he said all of it was fuzzy to him, it was at a time when he was just getting started. The magazine pages I sent him showed he did take the picture, but any photos and negatives were deep in his files somewhere, if he still had them. But I did have the print.

Today his website is awesome with architectural photos. He said something else that I relayed to my husband, Tom: Philip said writing a book was "quite an accomplishment." "I know," Philip said, "because my wife, Karen Melvin, just co-authored *The Legendary Homes of Lake Minnetonka*, and it was a tremendous amount of work. Really a labor of love to put together a book and I commend you for it."

I told Tom because I knew—Tom was in for it. Tom would have no use of the dining room table or the kitchen table for a very long time to come.

Those world records were about to come down on us.

11

On Air and on Paper

I f you have never tap-danced in an air-tight glass box not much bigger than you, done about twenty takes—making a radio commercial—it might be compared to playing half a soccer game on a hot day and being seen on a big screen the whole time—I would imagine.

"This fancy footwork is brought to you by the fine folks at S.R. Pasteur, La Salle Courtyard, downtown Minneapolis. Produced by Stewart & Stewart." But I never had heard my taps so clearly and I got to hear it many more times on radio.

Other solos were curious and startling. One day an artist asked to sketch me, for the *Minneapolis Star*. She sat in my classroom. Much less obtrusive than a camera, I soon forgot about her, even though there usually were no observers when I taught.

One day, I opened the *Minneapolis Star*: I was now a full-page color caricature on the cover of the "Taste" section. The artist signed her name LYNE//E.

I was like a pink flamingo on legs, bending forward in white top hat and tails on a hot-pink background. Every part of me was exaggerated in her drawing.

BIG!

I took it in, this extra me. I liked her. Somehow in all of this I'd created a character with a life of her own, one I didn't control, but one I caused.

The artist was having fun and causing fun, I thought. It was like going to Dayton's and having a personal shopper show me what I could be. Except this drawing ended up on display.

But it was fun. I had to be me without worrying or life would be gray.

By the end of the year another full-page color caricature of a tap dancer was on the back page of *Butler Square's Gazette*, only in black top hat and tails, by artist Robert Halliday. I was the Tapping Santa in the square that December, in black top hat and tails.

On Sunday March 19, *Ripley's Believe It or Not* ran a cartoon nationwide of Kristin and me when we were Tapping Minneapples. It was a sketch from a photo.

The picture that inspired the cartoon. Beth and Kristin as Minneapples. (Courtesy of *Skyway News*)

Some mothers scrapbooked. My mother scrap-*walled*. One by one, to my surprise, the newspaper caricatures of me took their place, on a pink stucco wall on the ground floor of her home, next to First Communion collages, Christmas family portraits, weddings. The whole production was reflected on a wall of mirrors. She was doing what mothers do.

But soloing can get lonely. I was gearing up to try another big event.

I remembered the day I proposed that everyone should dance for the opening of the arts center. It was a fascinating thought: couldn't my audience dance as well? Wouldn't they just love it?

12

The Flanagan Phenomenon
Going Boldface in Barbara

One of the thrills of a lifetime is the dozens upon dozens of times my name has been in boldface, and my event names, and their stars—in Barbara Flanagan's column, in the *Minneapolis Star*, from 1979 through today, literally today. I have to say that because it just is. She gave me a rhythm.

Looking back I am certain that the events I was to do sailed, flourished, on her say so.

And I would be of little use as an event planner, a publicist, an entertainer, if I didn't notice what people asked me, what they found of interest. And people asked, continually: "Why are you in Barbara's column so often?" Or "How do the events get in? And "You must know her well." "Are you related?" And "What is she like?"

It was a very big deal and people wondered. Unspoken, I know, was the curiosity: What is it like? How is it the day you are in? A respected columnist shares enormous power when she writes about us and what we do.

The fact is, I never met her in person for more than a moment, until her public retirement party, when she went from two columns a week to one a month. She was seeing many people that day, like a receiving line, but she was personable and oh, so quick. And, ever the reporter, she asked what the next thing might be.

BIG!

Basically, I think my connection to Barbara was simple—she and I wished for the same things. When what I was doing was in her column, I knew I had an event in the works that she wished to happen. Anyone who needs publicity to pull something off needs a media outlet with identical goals and values. Not close: nail it.

Did my events happen because Barbara mentioned them? It did seem so. It was that magical. At the least, once I mailed the news release and then saw it in her column—I knew that she suspected, trusted that something would indeed happen. I had a responsibility to come through. The best part: that she believed seemed to transfer power. It would be a good thing for the people and the city were my event to happen.

Really, the day I would have something in Barbara's column turned golden. Usually I was thick into organization and the notice gave me twenty-four hours of euphoria: my vision was out there, after months of my promises and hopes, my talking and typing. I could hold her column in my hand, an inkling that what I was about was real, as of that issue of the newspaper.

Like this: I always made a run through Lunds grocery store, because neighbors would stop to say those words: "I saw Barbara's today; now what is it you are up to?" On that day I couldn't run around the lake without stopping because someone would stop to hug and say, "There you go again. Now what is happening?" Like that. Of course, Lunds is like that, a little town. I ran into Walter Mondale in the canned vegetables aisle the day after the presidential elections. "I didn't know where else to go," he said, and I knew the feeling.

But besides the elation, everyone needs a hug when they work hard on a vision. No one ever solos, is alone, as much as the organizer of an event for a city or town or state. If anything goes wrong it is not no-fault. The organizer must step up.

But when what you are doing is for thousands who want to have fun, and for a client who wants to provide a good time that also connects to what they do—not be embarrassed—nothing works like having Barbara say you're on to something.

And many are out there doing interesting things. But when Barbara gets the word out, some of the good things happen. My Flanagan clippings covered a thirty-six-by-forty-eight-inch collage until I finally put them into a scrapbook, of the days.

BIG!

Barbara dispenses magic, the star-for-a-day kind, for the organizer and the client, awareness for her cities. And if the event that earns her nod comes through a smash, the city, the town, the street, the building becomes a wonderful place to be. A "Wow," as Barbara says.

I wonder if anyone else has written about how much fun it is to have what they are doing in her column. Or even if I should.

But I can't help it; it just is.

Beth and Barbara. (Courtesy of Barbara Flanagan, *Minneapolis Star Tribune*)

Three events in two years received a CUE Award from Minneapolis's Committee on the Urban Environment for improving the quality of life in the city. (Courtesy of Beth Obermeyer)

Part II

Record Breakers Take the Town

Marching Band to Leap Froggers, Bucket Passers to Break Dancers, Chorus Line to More Tap!

13

Finding the Way

After that Big Tap got into the Guinness book—for the next decade and a half or so—I was on fire. All around the beat of the solos went big events, and they broke more records. They came to be the handle for which I was known, although I did many smaller events that I loved, too, big in other ways. But somehow a good idea often seemed to get bigger, and then had to be handled with care; absolutely, there could be no flying by the seat of the pants.

Creativity like that came with great risk, unlike the security of the solos. But those world record events came off like drum rolls—bang! I think a lot about all those world records, and I treasure them through today, especially the people in them. I had grown up dancing out every night in my small town and that left me alone, out of the swing of school friends. When I did huge people events, me and my new friends rocked our towns.

In their time I let each event stand on its own, made my best call each time. Then, to cross over to the next big event—it was mysterious, always. I left full flight from something I'd never seen before. Losing myself tingled. I wanted that again and again. To spring from intuition and passion with an image—that's rich. But a risk. But rich.

Meanwhile I got called "The Guinness Lady." That was exciting but that was not it. In fact, all but two of the six records were not intentional Guinness, not at first. They started for their own reasons, grew out of the people and their territories. I didn't think I was "wacka-wacka," either, an article on the tenth anniversary of TA DA! Special Events, and in context it didn't sound mean. But I didn't dwell on that. "Event Guru?" Like I would know all, ever.

Great ideas sprang from a base and before they came I needed to find out everything about the company or group, their image, what had been said about them, what they needed, what they wanted to say. And, match it to a community need. Not just make the world's largest hamburger. The client was not a circus out to entertain.

Minneapolis Star columnist Barbara Flanagan gave me a different title each event. I listened. I "danced," I was a "special event consultant," and "a choreographer of crowds." That last one rang. It was the cross-over from dance to events.

Sometimes Barbara said I was "a producer," "staged a happening," even "created the spectacle."

When she got to the concept part, I did listen: I was "the inspiration behind the event," "a bright-idea woman," "behind eye-popping events." I was "famous for staging local extravaganzas" and "whopping events downtown." I created "happy mob scenes." She used action words like "rally . . . take charge . . . lure."

I took all of that away, armed myself. And this much was fact: the events got into the *Guinness Book of World Records* "for their scale and organization," she said.

After three world records, a *Minneapolis Star Tribune* writer (the *Star* and *Tribune* had become one paper by then) called. At the start of the interview—tucked cozy in a booth in Ichabod's, front corner of the Hennepin Center for the Arts—I measured my words. Reading about oneself in the paper can be hard. Some criticism—often it's just a handy show of wit with a bit of cynicism—no one can do a thing with that. Besides, behind typeface one can bite. People never say to someone's face what they might write when on a roll.

So I was cautious. But soon I talked up a storm with Jeff Strickler. The *Star Tribune* now had a face, and he was friendly. As my father always philosophized: "It's amazing what you say when you get to talking." (I took that to be a good thing.)

And late one afternoon, the paper arrived on my step. It was a full-page cover story in the Variety section. The headline: "World record expert puts fun first!" I didn't know I would say that going in but it sounded right. I didn't know it would be a huge article, either. I ripped to the second page: the headline: "RECORDS? You have to prove it!" Both headlines were dead-on. And then:

> Obermeyer has probably gotten the area more national TV coverage than even Walter Mondale . . . To her the event is the thing, not the record. If you want to put together an event that involves lots of people having lots of fun, call Obermeyer; if you want to see if you can eat a bicycle, save your quarter.

I rolled in the paper. Because this much was true: the fun we had—just celebrating the town, the people—could get big publicity. The city was a good place to be, these events said.

As time went by, Don Del Fiacco did a full column in the *St. Paul Dispatch* on each record. He said I "enthusiastically prowl our cities liveliest thoroughfares." And that was true; my events were all in big busy city streets. He nailed that.

Two ended up on streets through downtown Minneapolis, Hennepin and Marquette. Another went six miles down Lake Street. In St. Paul it was Frogtown. Another traveled three miles of the saintly city. The last one had thousands on Kellogg Boulevard, along the river. Smaller events claimed spots we wanted to own, too, like the day Bridgeman's Ice Cream Parlours planned a Loring Park Nutcracker of snow sculptures, in Loring Park—at the time not a family park, not at all. Think up that! So yes. The streets I loved had the heart of a city along their edge—neighborhoods with ethnic and economic ranges, great citizens and spirit when tapped.

But Del Fiacco had more:

"She is a . . . gregarious, record-setting—and entirely proper—woman of the streets . . . who lives quite grandly in Minneapolis's plush Kenwood District . . ."

Tom got a belly ache laughing at the lifestyle part. Our house—granted, it's historic and one house removed from Lake of the Isles—but it's family-sized, for an architect who could shore up the 100-year-old details, like windows that wouldn't shut.

More Del Fiacco. When a young woman called to say she was dancing on the street:

> She won't be undulating to the throb of "Night Train" at Augie's Theater Lounge, a saloon which has long been a refuge for fading exotic dancers . . . Her song: "Yankee Doodle Dandy." The audience: visitors to downtown Minneapolis. It might enliven the . . . loop area, a dreary sleazy thoroughfare once fueled elegantly by strippers Kandy Kane, Smokey Turner, and Lisa Depraved. "They're starting to fix up Hennepin, you know," Obermeyer says, noting the immense downtown renewal project.

I tried to absorb such humor in the moment, with the reservation that it was all more complicated than he thought. But I did need a bite of realism. A friend active in community fundraisers even asked: was all this my version of community service? Because as Tom said, often—I don't exactly have a get-rich-quick scheme going.

Still, in all the craziness and fun, the Big Tap inspired me. I held up every idea to that, to see how it was the same, how different.

What came into view in the emerging formula was the mixed crowd. If the event made any street safe and the people laid claim to it as well—if the community pulled together—I guess I created a good gang? Leaving its mark? As time passed I did see that crime didn't spring around those events. They were too blended with all kinds of people working together.

At the tenth year of my events, City Council's Barbara Carlson pumped me up:

> Your . . . productions and spectacles have enriched many lives . . . as a constructive advocate of many worthy causes (you) have proved an invaluable link between clients and community . . . and (you) remain a constant source of surprise and pleasure, fast becoming a Minneapolis institution.

I said this was a fairy tale and on some days it was. That letter hangs by my computer through today. It feels good to see work and efforts put into words by someone at the city. Most surely I had a brand. Most important though is how I felt about what I did.

TA DA! City Celebrations popped for a dozen years in all. Large-scale public events in surprising open spaces. And most of my events had something to do with the arts because arts soothe. All, I think, were truly one-of-a-kind. Some succeeded against all odds and advisement. In any case, I tried not to take reviews too seriously. Finally Barbara Flanagan gave me one that set me free: "Never underestimate Beth Obermeyer." But better if I didn't even think about it.

And this might seem to be enough about me but did I ever need to pull together. The me in events spoke for a client; I was them. They chose me. I was on a team, not solo. And I had a larger goal, and I was defining it as I went.

US Magazine did an article with my photo: Front Runner; "TA DA! She gives events a special flourish." The writer separated my events from a huge root beer float that spoiled in the sun and polluted the lake. Being mentioned alongside that reminded me that events grown big did have to be handled with care. Fun as they appeared, they brought serious logistic challenges. Colossal ones also needed careful coordination with Guinness.

And that has changed, monumentally. Today the Guinness book has a service online, includes assistance picking a category, a Guinness logo to use on posters and information, a person who comes to the event to verify. A fast track application—$450.

But in 1979 the process was by mail, the inquiry answered by mail from the London or New York office, with a list of requirements for the record chosen. The Guinness name was not to be used until the event went into the book.

David Boehm, the Guinness editor, was kind and helpful after I filed each event. Every June he called to let me know if our record was being challenged. The Guinness book had a personal touch. (Although when I asked permission to use a photo of the Guinness book and letters for this book, an editor answered from London, in ten days.)

For the record, I will start the list of record breakers I directed in the Twin Cities with the 1,801 tap dancers, to put that event in context with the tapping of the time: Rosie Radiator in Los Angeles; at BBC in London; in Perth, Australia. I did write a book on this event, *The Biggest Dance: A Miracle on Concrete*, North Star Press of Saint Cloud also, 2011.

The record-breaking events that followed continue the tale—a path to the Guinness book, yes—but, more important, a path by the people to claim their territories.

The World's Largest Tap Dance: 1,801; Minneapolis, a Single Routine, Rows LLL-QQQQQ. (Tom Sweeney. With the permission of the *Star Tribune*)

14

The Big Tap
The World's Largest
Tap Dance

1,801 Tap Dancers on Hennepin Avenue

The big tap dance sparked a light that never seemed to leave. They startled and entertained, and along with their crowd spread unbridled energy and joy. Briefly, the path to the *Guinness Book* included:

Record to break:
The 1979 Guinness book listed a tap record, set by Roy Castle: 500 tap dancers, in a routine on the *1977 Christmas Show* BBC-TV Center. That year the tap-dance record fell in the record book between Custard Pie Throwing and Demolition. The 1980 Guinness book: 528 tap dancers in Los Angeles from the Brenda Kalatzes Tap Studio, for the *Guinness Spectacular* TV transmission, ranging in age from four to eighty-four.

Our record:
The 1981 book: the greatest assemblage of tap dancers ever in a single routine is 1,801, organized by Beth Obermeyer for the TV program *Twin Cities Today*.

BIG!

We beat the previous record almost four times over. Perhaps we were inspired to such high numbers by the sentence at the end of the Guinness letter received prior to the event: "The figure you have to exceed is 528. We have received one or two letters recently expressing an interest in toppling this record."

We Stayed:

The 1982 Guinness book listed us again, this time adjusted to: "Dancing in unison in a whole routine, sponsored by the Minnesota Dance Theatre to open the Hennepin Center for the Arts."

The book used our *Minneapolis Star* overhead photo of the 1,801 tap dancers, by Regene Redniecki. It split the width of the Guinness page with a photo of a single belly dancer whose record was dancing for 110 hours.

What I still find amazing about our Big Tap is that every group who registered showed up with their predicted number or close to it, something I'd see again and again from Minnesotans.

Record Broken:

The Guinness book 1983: our record was broken, and not by New York, who claimed it every year in our paper. The record went back to BBC-TV show *Record Breakers*, led by Betty Laine, who broke our record by a measly 417. They counted and verified 2,218 tappers, performing at the Eastney Royal Marine Barracks in Portsmouth, England.

They stayed for the 1984 Guinness book.

In the 1985 book, the Guinness tap record was still not New York, although we again read in the paper that it was. In Concert Hall, Perth, Australia, 2,647 tap dancers appeared at the TVW7, annual telethon.

But by the 1986 book, it came back to America. Finally, it went to New York, who listed 3,450 tap dancers, sponsored by Macy's in New York City on Thirty-fourth Street.

The 1987 book: New York repeats, with more: 3,565 tap dancers.

Not that it matters, but the tappers are listed in Stunts and Miscellaneous Endeavors, now alphabetically between Cucumber Slicing and Diving, followed by Domino Toppling.

Tom said it: "Sometimes they just don't know what to think."

Sponsored by: The Minnesota Dance Theatre. The tappers appeared at the Hennepin Avenue Merchants Association Block Party, and opened Business Salutes the Arts Week, sponsored by the Downtown Council and the Greater Minneapolis Chamber of Commerce.

15

The World's Longest Bucket Brigade

8,676 people lined six miles of Lake Street, 76 blocks between the Mississippi River and Lake Calhoun, connecting 9 Minneapolis neighborhoods, 5 parks, 130 community groups

It wasn't even my idea, but I knew a winner when it was brought to me. I ran hard with it and was never disappointed. Bucket passing was not an art form, served no real purpose since pioneer times, but I thought it would ring. If the people came, that is. It was a test, an experiment: would Lake Street and its environs take up the call? And it was new for me: I wasn't in the group. I wasn't even leading it. I was directing only. Now the people stood on their own, the stars.

Record to Break: Guinness did not have this record listed in their book, and at the time they were unlikely to start a new category. They said they were publishing a book, not an encyclopedia, and that made sense.

Today any record application is considered for the Guinness book, but even when successful the majority of recognized world records do not appear in the book or even on their online site. The book has shifted, their

Internet site says, from "a text-oriented reference book to an illustrated product." But every recognized record holder is issued a certificate.

But even though at first Guinness said, in early 1981, that a bucket brigade would not be a record category, it was what the Lake Street Council wanted to do. A brigade could be a good link for the long, long bazaar.

First I rehearsed bucket passers and stop lights. Children on the Howe School playground took three minutes to pass the bucket one block, if it was half full. More water and it was too heavy and sloshed. I allotted three minutes per block, about two seconds per person

Bucket rehearsal, Howe School.

Next I timed the stoplights. Five light sequences on five corners would show red for about one minute. So seventy-six blocks times three minutes plus minutes for red stop lights equaled three hours and thirty-two minutes. I sent rehearsal photos to neighborhood newspapers.

My theory: if we are going to do something, we have to do it right. A light whimsical event deserved care. Besides, we always had to consider the safety and comfort of the people.

Next I asked the fire department to provide a truck to follow the bucket on its route, to make its progress larger than life. I would ride the truck and pause the bucket at corners, or speed it up as needed, to keep it on schedule. The fire department committed, unless there was a fire nearby.

Big!

Months out, I walked the seventy-six blocks. I asked one business owner on each of the blocks to be block captain, wear a fireman's hat at the event, and collect the signatures of each bucket passer and mail them to me afterwards. I controlled the event by telling each business what time the bucket would hit their block within the almost six-mile march.

And then I called, visited, mailed to every group I could find, from a rowing club, block club, tennis center, singles group, Sons of Norway, Little Brothers of the Poor, Northwestern Bell, dance school, church . . . every park. And please, tell a neighbor. I went to the Sabathani Center and other backbone organizations with Charleen Bacigalupo, overall Bazaar chairman. I personally delivered flyers to each of the schools, chose a different three to visit each Friday morning, and chatted with each school secretary, I'd watch until the flyers got stuffed into the mail boxes, to go home with children.

Each block captain was asked to reserve 100 people on their block, about one per yard, and sign in any who appeared that day. Some blocks had an easier time than others—a cemetery ran for blocks on Lake Street—but they'd space out the people they got; they'd run the bucket between persons if necessary. At any rate, some blocks had hundreds coming.

The day arrived, a beautiful sunny day. Senator David Durenburger started the first bucket, supposedly the only bucket, after receiving it from the Rowing Club, who had rowed it across the river from their site. Councilman Martin Sabo also started a bucket, just in case. The plan went without a flaw. Some blocks swelled to 500 people. I strained from my high spot on the fire truck to see where the bucket was going in the crowd. It was sometimes very hard to see. But it always emerged at the curb at the end of the block, water intact.

Sometimes I thought a street-sized wave of water was washing down Lake Street. As the bucket crossed the intersection, the arms went up, the cheering soared, a block at a time. And with each street crossing we left behind a party.

A photo of each block was taken by Charleen and also of the events she had placed on all major intersections. I made a collage so I could see them all at once. Also riding the truck was Lake Street Council President Herb Whittemore.

Some blocks had tap dancers from a school. Some had bar patrons.

BIG!

Collage of Lake Street during the World's Longest Bucket Brigade. (Charleen Bacigalupo, courtesy of Charleen Bacigalupo, collage Beth Obermeyer)

On Lake Street during the bucket passing. (Charleen Bacigalupo, courtesy of Charleen Bacigalupo)

Churches, families, bike store patrons, everyone that store-fronted on Lake Street or lived in the neighborhood was out that day. A driver's license center. Hair salon. The banks on Lake Street had strong efforts. An antique store, shoe store, flower store, art materials store. Used car salesmen and customers. It was easy for them to take part because they knew what time the bucket would hit their block, within five minutes.

People elbowed and slid and stood on tiptoe to see. They cheered, roller skated and hula hooped while they waited on the long stretch of inner city street. No water was spilled and the original bucket was joined by many more, plus a few frogs. The photos of the people on each of the seventy-six blocks appeared to move to the far corners of the world and back. The energy and camaraderie I saw from my perch on the accompanying fire truck! If only the people, the street, could hold this spirit tight forever.

Of all the record breakers, this one spoke to me the most, perhaps because it went on so long and sprang from so many neighborhoods. And proved—even with only the rhythm of a bucket passing hand to hand, it made music. I liked observing, not dancing this time. I saw it all.

Because the bucket did arrive at the lake on schedule at 3:32, three hours and thirty-two minutes in play after the noon start. It was tap-danced to the water's edge, and people not physically able to stand and run awaited in kayaks. They paddled the buckets out about twenty feet and dumped the water to a roar of the crowd and many cameras.

All three local TV stations covered the riotous community celebration on Lake Street, as well as the local programs, *KSTP Twin Cities Today*; *What's New on WTCN*; *Incredible Kids on WCCO*. Radio hosts Steve Cannon and Boone & Erickson on WCCO-AM and Charlie Bush on KSTP radio. The two big papers in Minneapolis and St. Paul did stories before and after, with photos. The *Twin Cities Reader* ran seven pages of photos, an article and a list of 120 community groups and the times they were reserved on seventy-six blocks. *Skyway News*. Barbara Flanagan, almost one third of her *Star* column.

Don Del Fiacco included all the facts—how to enroll in the brigade, the elaborate logistics. He also said Lake Street "is a place where joy long has been a drop in the bucket." And "Obermeyer is certain . . . the bucket will be passed smoothly, safely and spectacularly." And that I was "saving Tom for a crisis." I did say all of that. The publicity was large. Both Charleen and I put out information, her for the bazaar in general, and also the bucket brigade, the opening event—I for the bucket brigade, also the logistics of the bazaar. And businesses on Lake Street promoted their part as well.

After comparing a visual count—which could not be absolutely accurate where the crowd filled the sidewalks and into the street—but not misleading either because it closely matched the signatures—I sent the record to Guinness: 8,676 people, along with verification from important people. One hundred signatures collected by the block captain at Midas Muffler Shops did blow away in the next day's storm, but we had a photo of his block and were confident we could count the Midas block.

Cleo Dvoracek, bazaar chairman, in her documentation for Guinness, wrote:

> I rode on the fire truck and saw all walks of life: the high school with over 200 students in T-shirts, the handicapped brought in a bus to participate, families with their children, business owners with their employees, nursery schools, dance schools, and many, many more. The bucket brigade will be a lasting memory in this area.

But the record attempt, fabulous as it was in numbers and energy, documented as it was by photos in papers and on television—national news by 6:00 p.m.—was still discouraged by Guinness. "Not everybody has the facilities," their letter said. I assumed they meant lakes, not buckets.

We knew this ahead of time, and we did it anyway. Our mission was larger than getting in the book.

And that summed it up. Guinness responded quickly. "We have received the Bucket Brigade material and are studying what to do with it."

Alas, nothing was done with it, for a while anyway.

But that bit of "nothing is happening" news from Guinness never even hit our newspaper. By then Lake Street had 8,676 stars, covered grandly at their time. They were like a quirky orgy before the next day's storm.

Sadly, three years later, another letter came: "Since a bucket brigade is too close to our human chain record, which is larger, we cannot accept your record." Our materials were returned. But it wasn't over yet, not at all. We held tight, waited.

Meanwhile, for the record, the following list of participants—the groups on the street by block—is a word photo of the neighborhoods around Lake Street. It started at the Mississippi at Forty-sixth Street and ended at Lake Calhoun.

11:00 a.m.: Mississippi River

Forty-seventh: Minneapolis Rowing Club; Captain Mike Kapra, River Lake Standard Station;

Forty-sixth: Minnehaha Academy; Captain Doug Barends, Import Auto Specialist;

Forty-fifth: Cooper School; Captain Maureen Glance, Duling Optical;

Forty-fourth: Home School

Forty-third: Elmer the Tree, Minneapolis Park and Recreation Board; Captain Jim Kirkholm, Honda Town;

Forty-second: Meriam Park, St. Paul; Sanford School; Captain Dr. C. McDougall, E. Lake Animal Clinic;

Forty-first: Deeann Dance; Nativity Soft Ball; Gohl Family, St. Paul; Captain Loren Blixt, Taco Bell;

11:30:

Fortieth: Captain David Lerner, East Lake Liquor;

Thirty-ninth: Captain Shirley Dalton, Star Beauty;

Thirty-eighth: Captain Russ Bankson, Bankson-Almquist Agency, Inc.;

Thirty-seventh: Captain Mark Enderlin, True Value Hardware;

Thirty-sixth: Mary Ruth Dance Studio; Longfellow Park; Rusty Grand, Butler Drug;

Thirty-fifth: Mary Ruth Dance; Captain Doug Bush, Northwest Inst. of Medical Lab. Technique;

Thirty-fourth: Free School; Captain Carol Blair, Soderberg Florists;

Thirty-third: St. Albert the Great Parish and School;

Thirty-second: Brown Institute, Captain Dick Hanson, Brown Institute;

12 noon
Thirty-first: South Parks Consolidated;
Thirtieth: Roosevelt High School Cheerleaders and Rockettes Danceline; Captain Denny Dahl, Big Wheel Auto;
Twenty-ninth: First Bank Minnehaha; Captain Davis Noteboon, First Bank Minnehaha;
Twenty-eighth: Seward School; Captain Vince Kumerow, The Lake Street Bootery;
Twenty-seventh: Captain Myron Handeland, the Pizza Company;
Minnehaha: Hiawatha YMCA;
Snelling: Shari Sinn's School of Dance, Shakopee;
Hiawatha: Jill Sinn's Eden Prairie Dance Arts Center;
Twenty-third: North Country American Volleyball Association; Folwell School;
Twenty-second: Folwell School;
Twenty-first: Corcoran Park, Block Club;
Twentieth: South High School; Captain Theresa Borah, Clark Oil & Refining Company;
Nineteenth: Little Brothers of the Poor; Sibley Park; Captain Michael Henley, Little Brothers of the Poor;

12:48
Cedar: Cedar Lake Florists, Captain Arne Raymond;
Eighteenth: Mike Mika, Cedar Lake Car Wash;
Seventeenth: Girl Scouts; Heart of the Beast Puppet; Salvation Army; Capt. Roger Suneson, Music Center;
Sixteenth: The City Youth Center; Captain Tom Nolan, First Bloomington Lake National Bank;
Bloomington: Bancroft Neighborhood Association; Dick Earl, Butler Drug;
Fifteenth: Bancroft School; Captain Dave Gannon, Mr. Gatti's;
Fourteenth: Sabathani Center; Disney's Table Tennis Center;
Thirteenth: Powderhorn Park Neigh. Association;

1:16
Twelfth: Elliot Park Neighborhood, Inc.;

Eleventh: Marquette Lake Bank, Captain Lavonne Peterson; Marquette Bank, Captain Dale Harris;
Eleventh: Phillips Neigh. Imp. Ass; Abbott NW Hospital; Captain Elmer Nelson, Narum Shoes;
Elliott: Sister Kenney Institute; Deeann's Dance Studio, Deephaven, Wilder C.;
Chicago: Phelps Park; Captain Orville K. Rassett, Chicago Lake Florist;
Columbus: Knights of Columbus, #435, Captain Bob Parker;
Oakland: Wilder B; Captain Jim Fudali, Midas Muffler;
Portland: Wilder A; Captain Joseph E. Baker, Senior Citizen Club;

1:52
Fifth: Captain Tim Jordan, Jordan Realty;
Fourth: Central Neighborhood Association; Captain Lee Lathrup, Hirshfield's Paint;
Clinton:
Third: Reachout; Captain Merrill Anderson, Reachout;
Second: Martin Luther King Park;
Stevens: Mpls. Campfire Girls, Mpls Techical College; Captain Alex Stazely, Church's Chicken;
First: K-Mart; Captain Paul Feller, K-Mart;
Nicollet: Super Valu; Northwestern Bank; Captains Rod Martin, Sam Morrison;
Blaisdell: YMCA, Urban West Central; Captain Guy Berg, The Karate Chop;
Pillsbury: Lyndale Neighborhood Association; Captain Ozzie Haas, Haas Display;
Pleasant: Incarnation School & Parish;

2:28
Grand: Whittier Park; Sunbeam Appliances; Captain Linda Schatzlein, Schatzlein's Western;
Harriet: Painter Park; Lake Country School; Captain Paul Williams, Paul Williams Tire Co.;

Garfield: Sunsight Books; Whittier Alliance; Captain Herb Delott, Sunsight Books;

Lyndale: Northwestern Bell; Art Materials; Captain Dick Nelson, AARCEE Rental;

Aldrich: TC Sidebanders (CB'S); The Fed; Super America; Captain Tim Moen, Custom Camera;

Bryant: Roller Skaters; Captain Lynda McHale, The Corner Store;

Colfax: Roller Skaters; Captain Julie Bloor, Blue Heron Café;

Dupont: The Children's Museum;

Emerson: Minnesota Zoo; Garden of Eden; Rainbow Café;

Hennepin: Sons of Norway; Captain Diane Schmidt, Over the Rainbow;

Holmes: Supporters of Salute to the Disabled.

3:32 LAKE CALHOUN!

Our Record:

And then, surprise! The record went into the British version of the book! The first news came from a friend of my brother, Bob. He saw the listing in London, heard about it on the radio. I love word-of-mouth, the most successful events have it. Several years later it was confirmed. It was a long journey, but Lake Street arrived, as though they didn't know that already. What I noted was that the event wasn't dance or music while it definitely had a rhythm.

I notice not a lot of dialogue in my tale for the bucket brigade. Organizing can be a lonely occupation as well. But mostly, I suspect, I just don't remember vivid details like I did in the Big Tap. The Big Tap event immersed me in dance and tap, and as Barbara Flanagan said about my first book *The Biggest Dance*, "Beth Obermeyer loves tap dance and it shows."

But even though I was not dancing, I was organizing and watching, reveling in it all. And I might like that job most of all, I came to realize during this event. Not as much into my wiring, perhaps, but I could step back better and really see the magic.

I was making the step from solo to leading to directing. I wasn't submerged and that might be a good thing for the event.

BIG!

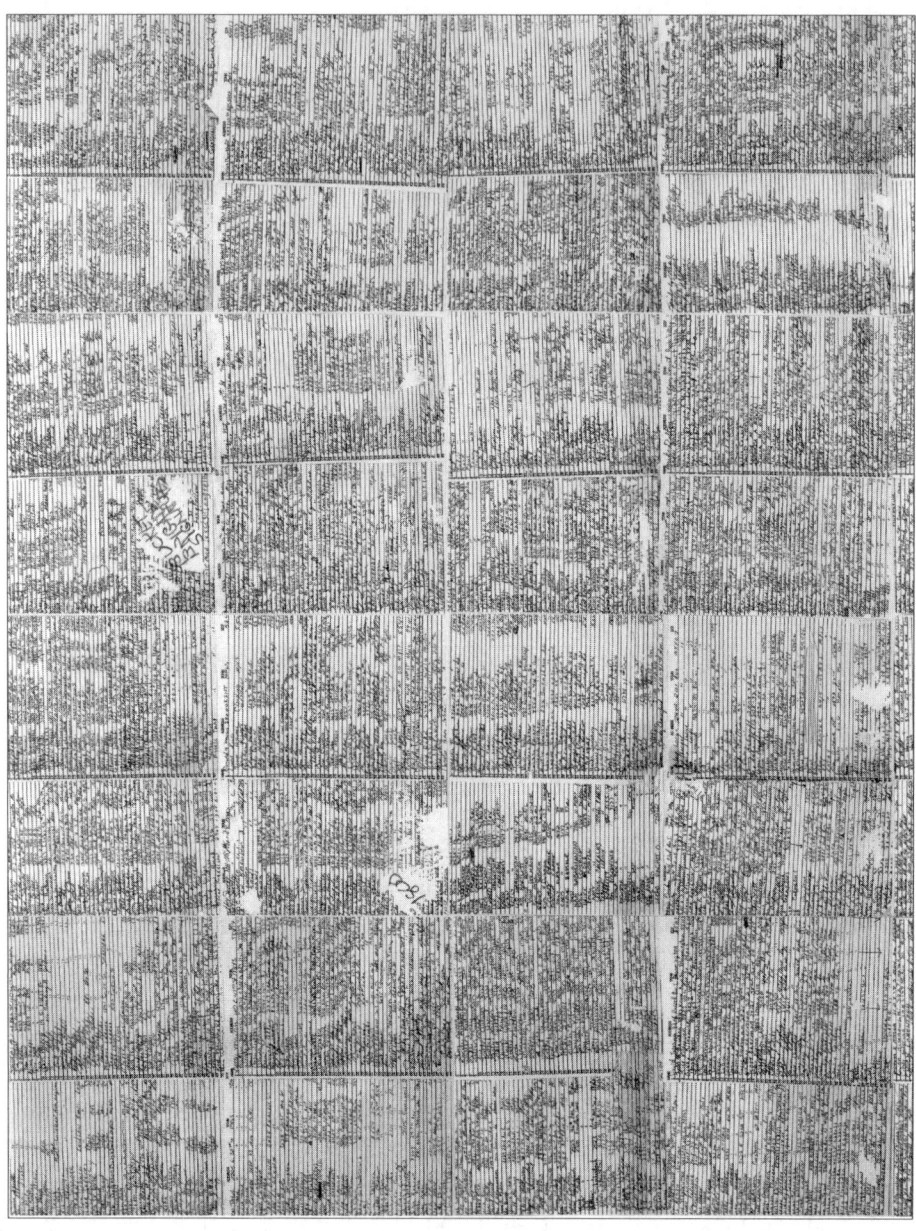

Sample: less than 1,800 of the 8,500+ signatures taken at the World's Longest Bucket Brigade. (Beth Obermeyer)

16

The World's Largest Marching Band

2,512 marching musicians and 494 flag bearers,
baton twirlers, and banner carriers.
Conducted by Dr. Frank Bencriscutto, University of
Minnesota Director of Bands.
Guest-conducted by eighty-year-old Meredith Willson,
composer of *The Music Man.*

The Big Band record went into the Music section of the Guinness book. This one had a sophisticated charm all its own. It happened two years to the day after the Big Tap: back we went to the downtown streets of Minneapolis, just four months after the bucket brigade. Student musicians statewide, from Canada to the Iowa border, all pulled together.

Now I might have been in over my head. I'd not been in a marching band. In fact, my instrument was the piano.

At first I wanted to recruit the public, anyone with an instrument. But in talking to band directors, the better plan was to limit the challenges we faced doing the impossible—to stretch out a marching band sound for three blocks. We decided to include only existing bands, and connect them tightly.

Besides, marching musicians knew how they should look and sound on a street. Anyway, this time I was the organizer of the Big Band, not the conductor. The challenge was to find the best director for the musicians and allow his lead.

I also imagined using the outer lane for musicians in wheelchairs. Marquette has a lane separated by a curb and I thought they would be safe as they rolled and would add a great deal. But that lane ended up to be the lane for each band director to march alongside their band. Banners for each band also stretched across it.

The Big Band would not have the wild everyone of the tap dancers or the spontaneity. Even with this tight plan, Anne Brataas at the *St. Paul Pioneer Press* described what we saw: "The mega-band was a riot of gold braid, glitter, flags, and feathers that looked like a giant segmented insect holding the city under a siege of sound." I liked that.

Record to Break: 1,976 marching musicians, fifty-four drill majors, flag bearers, directors, in a two mile march down Pennsylvania Avenue, Washington, D.C., in 1973, Nixon's inaugural parade.

At the start, I took the idea to Maureen Wright, director of Special Events at Dayton's. Maureen was also chair of events at the Downtown Council. She sat at a great desk with a view of the city on one side and a wall of mirrors on the other.

Was this for real? It's what her eyes said. First she tied in Dayton's Jubilee Sale. The band would be on the ads. The store even sponsored a half-hour television show on the band with their ad. I signed a contract with the Downtown Council. The Big Band would open the second Business Salutes the Arts Week, as the Big Tap had the first.

Being from Mason City, Iowa, I contacted Meredith Willson, The Music Man, and asked him to direct. He said no. His advice: find the band director in our area with the greatest expertise for such a monumental task.

And that was only one person: Dr. Frank Bencriscutto, director of Bands, University of Minnesota. He was in contact with schools, statewide. They adored him and respected him.

I did, too, from the moment I met him. "Beth," he said. "What makes you take this on?" I didn't ask him the same question for fear he would change his mind. Large events had a way of exploding with details once they started to come off the proposal paper. I prepared a ten-page letter that included an information sheet, time, place, all the details needed. Maureen's event department gave it an edit. The marchers would be accepted in the order they applied, Dr. Ben said, and they ended up representing twenty-seven communities between the Canadian and Iowa borders of Minnesota. They ranged from large powerhouse bands to the prides of smaller towns, all fully ready.

Soon we'd gathered something of beauty, all those musicians coming together. Cromwell, Minnesota, population 181, who ordinarily "can't use the athletic field to march and are afraid of the nearby highway"—according to their registration form—decided to march through downtown Minneapolis anyway. But they wondered if their one-row band was enough. They were thinking fifteen musicians might be three rows. But we needed rows of fifteen to condense the sound.

Dr. Ben loved the Cromwell band, their spirit. He pointed out that the Cromwell banner along the edge of their band would be the same size as the banners of larger bands.

And rows as wide as fifteen did turn out to be difficult, hard to keep straight. "They start curling and get all messed up," said marcher Scott Thompson, in the *St. Paul Pioneer Press*.

One of the largest bands in the area declined. The director told me that if this were only someplace else—like Florida—they would do it. But plenty of others bands came on board. We even created a list of twenty bands as back-up, in case any canceled. And as it turned out, we were challenged, down the line.

Because close to the day of the march, their loyalty was challenged. Eden Prairie, among others, had a teachers' strike, including the band director. But parents of that band rallied, had fundraisers, hired their own buses and escorted their band themselves. Their band director ran the parade route alongside but behind the crowd, shadowing the buildings, anonymous.

Barrett, Minnesota, a smaller town, registered an amazing forty-five band members, who we came to notice—included ten-year-olds. Dr. Ben said that kind of spirit made our big band the best.

Beth's dining room tables with World's Largest Marching Band music, late at night. (Courtesy of Beth Obermeyer)

I dealt with organization, and Dr. Ben worked on the music problems of such a band. He had the music specially arranged by Red McLeod. And that music got sorted for three days and nights on long tables down my living room and across the dining room. A concert after the march was planned.

Beth's letters from Meredith Willson. (Courtesy of Beth Obermeyer)

Dayton's Maureen Wright and her committee of Downtown Council volunteers arranged to meet Meredith Willson at the airport. They placed special seating for dignitaries at the concert after as well as a reception for Meredith after the concert—events around the event.

I asked Northwestern Bank to adjust the Weather Ball on top of their building to blink in time with the music. Ordinarily the ball, since 1949, had blinked in agitation for precipitation. (And turned green for no change, red for higher, white for snow.) It was not an easy fix but they did it. Every video camera caught the phenomenon, I noticed after.

As for Meredith Willson, he received seven letters of invitation from me. The first six came back a polite, "No." But in the seventh letter, I found yet one more tact.

I did not know why he was saying no. The event was so perfect for the music man, nearing the end of his career. So I asked him only to guest-conduct his "Seventy-Six Trombones," in a concert after the march. And ride in a convertible before the Big Band. I enclosed the shiny white press kit that Dayton's provided with the band logo on the front and my press releases inside.

He accepted by return mail. Western Airlines agreed to fly the Music Man First Class; The Marquette Hotel housed him right on the Marquette parade route.

I loved the support. I went to a Downtown Council meeting with a strip of foam board three inches wide and a yard long, showing the colors of the bands in stripes, proportionate to how the band would look when three blocks long. For the Peavey Plaza concert, I colored another map by the color of the uniforms, showing reserved spaces for each band. And the real thing didn't look much different from atop. We even requested a uniform from each band to be displayed behind glass in the government center. Everyone loved seeing how such a band might look. It defied the imagination, and that was the fun.

Dave Moore, emcee for the World's Largest Marching Band concert (Courtesy of Dave Moore)

For the concert after, Minnesota Orchestra's conductor Henry Charles Smith soloed on his euphonium. Church bells rang with the final piece, and blanks fired from the roof of Orchestra Hall for the *1812 Overture*.

The towns and their schools were listed in alphabetical order (but accepted in the order received) and their names were chanted by emcee WCCO-TV's Dave Moore.

They were: Barrett; Big Lake; Bloomington, Kennedy; Bloomington, Lincoln; Braham, Westview; Burnsville;

Coon Rapids; Cromwell; Eden Prairie; Elk River; Elmore; Grey Eagle; Hastings; Hopkins, Eisenhower and Hopkins; Lindbergh; La Crescent; Minneapolis, Edison; Minneapolis, Southwest; Minnetonka; Montgomery; New Brighton; Irondale; New Hope Cooper; Norwood Central; Plymouth, Wayzata; St. Paul, Cretin; St. Paul, Highland; St Paul, Humboldt; Silver Lake; Spring Valley; South St. Paul; and Waterville, Waterville-Ellysian.

And . . . the University of Minnesota!

Last-minute drama had more schools on teacher's strike, but we were still big enough for the record, down 500 to about 2,500 but still 500 over the old record.

Alternate bands waited on stand-by, but the numbers did not go down enough to act. The back-up bands included:

Little Falls, Two Harbors, St. Paul Central, Gaylord, Eden Valley, St. Peter, Grand Meadow, Hector, Stewart, Sandstone, St. Paul, and Chaska.

As time drew close, we knew we'd need no more than a dozen back-up bands at the most. Their dedication was important in making certain the band succeeded.

The sound? Fortunately we did not have to do our rehearsal indoors, in the armory, if it rained.

And I was on MPR at 7:00 a.m. that morning and it was raining. The host over-dubbed a few dozen recordings to get an idea of the sound of so many bands. But by 10:00 a.m. the low October sun came over the plaza and the gold buttons blazed.

The effect of endless music, the director in an elevated bucket, passing just barely under skyways across the route—breathtaking. It stretched for blocks.

The next morning Meredith's face was on *Good Morning America*, his chant under puffs of breath. His eyes spun in ecstasy as he chanted: "Whatta band; Whatta band; Whatta band."

But soon, not quite to the end of directing, he turned to his wife, Rosemary, and the cameras shut down. He wanted to go home, to nearby Mason City, Iowa. He died not long after, but not before he directed one more time, the next January at the Rose Bowl, for his beloved Iowa Hawkeye band.

BIG!

World's Largest Marching Band rehearsal, Peavey Plaza. Maureen Wright and Beth on either side of Dr Ben (Philip Prowse, courtesy of Downtown Council)

Our Record:

Into the 1983 book: 2,512 marching musicians and 494 baton twirlers, flag bearers, and directors who played and marched in Minneapolis, Minnesota, on October 12, 1981.

The publicity went around the world and so did we. Charles Kuralt did a story on his television show. The *Washington Post*: "Meredith Willson led the big parade, not on Broadway but in downtown Minneapolis." And "IT WAS A SMASH!" Ken Wahlstad, managing director, International Festivals Association.

Eleanor Powell saw it on television. "Wow!" she wrote. "That was some band—I wish I had it in my *Born to Dance* (film) finale—imagine con-

Band assembled at 10:00 a.m. for rehearsal.

ducting from a cherry picker. I'd love to see that." I loved that she related to what we were doing.

Dave Moore said: "The star of the big band was Logistics! If the music itself was inspiring, it was no more so than the very fact that it was all there!"

We Stay:
Our record stayed in the 1984 Guinness book as well.
Challenge:
A man wrote Guinness to say that he was in a larger band, Speedway, Indiana, in 1924. "John Philip Sousa conducted 2,800 musicians." His letter was in the *StarTribune*.

I checked the Indianapolis newspaper. They found no such band reported in their files. The issue was dropped by Guinness for lack of evidence. Also, in his letter, he did not say the band marched, part of the record requirement.

BIG!

World's Largest Marching Band, led by flags, batons, banners. (Courtesy of *Skyway News*. Photo selected for *Guinness Book of Records*)

BIG!

Record Broken:
In the 1985 Guinness book: 2,560 musicians, in an official state parade, Kuala Lumpur, Malaysia. The whole parade contained 25,000 musicians and marchers.

In the 1986 book: 3,182 marching musicians, with 1,342 majorettes, from the Los Angeles area. They marched in Dodgers Stadium prior to a baseball game and were directed by Danny Kaye. Since stadiums have a limit of space, I assume they marched through the playing field and out, never all marching in the stadium at once. Or marched in until they formed a massed standing band? A stadium is too small for such a band to move forward. Our band was three blocks long and this band was one-third larger.

So when the Super Bowl came to Minnesota, I proposed we put the World's Largest Tap Dance and the World's Largest Marching Band together at half-time. I had the experience to do it and the standing band record showed they'd accept something that corralled, in a stadium. I had a pop-up artist do three moments in the half-time for the proposal, to show it 3-D. The response: "Your idea for Young America singing group may be appropriate for the pre-game. Please contact us."

I didn't. They apparently mixed up proposals. Mine was band and dance. I was certain they would not put that as a pre-game feature. I don't remember what they did, but today Super Bowl half-times tend to be solo performances by celebrities on a stage in the center of the field. My favorites will always be the ones that allow the people to take the field, make patterns. The thousands at the Sarajevo Olympics opening who made the patterns of traditional ski sweaters, the image lives for them forever. At any rate, helicopters could not fly over the Metrodome and that's what monumental productions needed.

Sponsored by:
Downtown Council of Minneapolis and the Greater Minneapolis Chamber of Commerce; Business Salutes the Arts Week, October, 1981.

M<small>Y MOMENT, SEPARATE FROM THE EVENT</small> took my breath away. It happened before Meredith Willson was even out of the airport.

I grew up down the street from Meredith, in Mason City, Iowa. We had the same accompanist, he in 1917, me in the mid-forties, fifties. But when he came to Minneapolis for our big event—nearing eighty years old—I didn't expect him to remember.

I wiggled as I waited for him to get off the plane. Our moment arrived. He took my hand with a grand sweep. Did music forever charge through him? His eyes were heightened, vivid, somehow young. He bowed, kissed my hand! He'd come out of his world for one electric moment and it was with me.

I didn't breathe, just reveled in the moment. I did suspect Rosemary, his wife, helped us along. She whispered in his ear, possibly our accompanist's name, and mine. We suspended in our moment, holding hands without words. But his true love called from across the room—the marching band, there to welcome him.

The story is so large I cannot fit it in this book. My times with him in my home town, pre-television, where live entertainment was served up like dessert, frame it. I title it: *The Days of Song and Lilacs*, because we all had volumes of both; song and lilacs had everything we needed and everyone had them.

World's Largest Band concert, Peavey Plaza. (Thomas Obermeyer)

17

The Great Shake

**12,314 hand shakers
Governor's Mansion to the State Capitol,
to shake the political candidate's hand**

The fourth district Republican Party had the idea. I liked it. But soon I found I'd never done an event that had an enemy, the other party. Dancers and bands had only friends.

Bill James was the shaker, running for Congress in the fourth District, St. Paul, against four-time incumbent Bruce Vento. Regardless of how I voted, I did think Bill needed name recognition. He had two first names. He was twenty-seven years old, new in politics. He was a West Point graduate and a viable candidate. He'd create a rhythm for miles with his shake.

And we did find shakers so leaning in every group. Thousands met the opponent of a four-time incumbent in a short time, fun and personal, with a downbeat.

Record to Break:
Teddy Roosevelt, 8,513 hands at a state occasion at the White House.

BIG!

At first the Guinness Book discouraged Bill James's try because they liked the existing record. "We have always stated that this record is not really open to competition. It is a historical record and not set up intentionally. "Outside public life the record tended to become meaningless because people wittingly or unwittingly shake the same hands repetitively," they said. But that didn't mean a candidate meeting so many people was not a good idea. We did it anyway.

So on a beautiful fall day, James walked the route, shaking 12,314 hands, giving each a button: "I met Bill James." Each block—for the most part—was reserved by a group, including the Left-Handers Association to college Young Republican groups. Boosting the shake count was the Dan Fogelberg concert that let out of the Convention Center towards the end of his route. Children in flag costumes got signatures. This event was unusual in that it connected people by touch.

Bill James shaking hands. The Great Shake. (Beth Obermeyer. Photo selected for *Guinness Book of World Records*. Courtesy of Beth Obermeyer)

Bill James was not elected, but the papers were kind: "There is only one candidate here who is any great shakes." And "Campaign in the fourth turns gripping indeed," said the *Minneapolis Star Tribune*. "A lot of shaking going on in the fourth district," said the *St. Paul Pioneer Press*. We sent the signatures and photos of every block to Guinness. The London office replied: "We will certainly keep the information regarding Mr. James on file but I am afraid we cannot undertake to include an entry."

We sent a photo of Mr. James with two children in flag costumes anyway.

Within a week the New York office of Sterling Publishing Company sent a letter: ". . . your submission of the handshaking record for Bill James has been accepted for inclusion in the *1984 Guinness Book of World Records*." They listed both Bill James and Roosevelt's records.

Our Record:
"Bill James of St. Paul, Minn. Shook hands with 12,314, 4-miles-long, for almost 9½ hours on Oct. 16, 1982."

Mr. James might not have been elected, but he did meet the people.
Sponsored by: The Independent Republican Party, Fourth District, Minnesota.

18
The World's Longest Tap Dance

4.1 miles, by 22 tap dancers

It went into the Theatre section of the Guinness book.
The Minneapple was the client of Brum and Anderson Public Relations. The city of Minneapolis adopted it as its official logo, at groundbreakings and celebrations. Give the apple legs—that's where I came in. It was a short jump of concept to have it tap-dance. I didn't intend to dance it myself, but my family was in Europe until the apples made their first appearance. So Kristin and I would be the Minneapples the moment we got home.

Owner Josh Levinson had us measured for Minneapple costumes before we left. As luck had it, on the flight home, the Andrew Sisters version of "Don't Sit Under the Apple Tree" was on the plane's sound system every half hour. Kristin and I rehearsed, in our headsets, in the tiny space outside the plane bathroom. The day we landed we were off and running, joined by twenty-seven more Minneapple tappers in shorts and T-shirts. The beat of the city's logo took the streets.

Record to Break:
None was listed in the category of distance tap dancing. But an article in a newspaper said Rosie Radiator, eternally tapping in San Francisco, had set a distance tap record.

Big!

I had not intended to set a tap distance record, but when I realized the parade route was almost as long as Rosie's effort—well, if I started the tap in the line-up, our record could be be 4.1 miles. The apple owner liked the idea.

Unfortunately, the parade day was ninety-one degrees and seventy-six percent humidity. We did it anyway. The Tapping Minneapple 4.1 mile effort was sent to the Guinness book.

I received a letter from David Boehm, Guinness editor: "I would like very much to know what the previous distance record was for tap dancing, if there was any. This is not a category that I think is being competed in."

I did think Rosie Radiator tapped across San Francisco but he didn't seem to have that information. Or even want the category because I had read Rosie had contacted them. We did it for fun anyway, and I am sure Rosie Radiator had a great deal of fun too. They were the Market Street Tappers and used drum sticks on manhole covers to keep the rhythm.

Amazingly, our record did go in; twenty-two of the twenty-seven starting dancers survived the heat. We never stopped tap dancing, never even marched, always did tap steps, which was a lot like jumping rope 4.1 miles. But that was the Guinness requirement. I list all twenty-seven starters; five were pulled, so close, just before the end, by Aquatennial officials trained to spot heat exhaustion.

Jennifer Buzelle, Debbie Lazar, Rebecca Orman, Camille Hankes, Sue Streed, Lisa Hayes, Chrissy O'Brien, Kristen Malmberg, Leslie Chapman-Lee, Jerry Hoffman, Gayle Peterson, Judy Larson Berry, Elizabeth Persico, Jennifer Kral, Laura Gilmer, Wendy Gilmer, Laurel Conviser, Donna Amundson, Lisa Beller, Vanessa Carlson, Deanna Carlson, Linda Reichow, Ellen Shulman, Amy Shulman, Laurence Shulman, and Peggy Seipp.

We didn't know it then but Peggy Seipp was to become MDT's premiere ballerina in years to come, our longtime Sugar Plum Fairy.

We Stay:
We go into the 1986 Guinness book as well.

This record also became a cartoon in *Ripley's Believe it or Not* syndicated cartoons, world-wide, separate from the Ripley's television show.

Ripley's cartoon of the Minneapples, part of the Longest Tap Dance. (Ripley's Believe It or Not®, © Ripley Entertainment, Inc., used with permission)

The feat also appeared as a math problem in the grade three to four textbook, *Grammar Rules*, an example of agreement of verbs with compound subjects: "Beth Obermeyer and her daughter Kristin hold a record for long-distance tap-dancing."

When the giant costumes disappeared after an appearance at St. Anthony Main shopping center—which was curious because it required a pick-up truck to move them, not because of their weight but their size—*USA Today* ran the *Tapping Minneapple* photo: "Hard Core Crime?"

Soon after the city changed to a red carpet as their official logo. But we'd had a lot of fun, Kristin and I, and the city logo went places the red carpet never could.

Record Broken:

The 1987 Guinness book; it is Rosie's turn. She led eleven dancers and danced 5.4 miles across San Francisco from Union Square to Ghirardelli Square. Rosie has now set up a year-round training program for distance tapping. She has developed and requires several kinds of distance tap shoes, to be changed during scheduled breaks. She also has designed the dance to minimize strain to the body.

Sponsored by:

The Minneapple, Josh Levinson owner.

19

The World's Longest Chorus Line

516 dancers, in the Metrodome
Twenty-fifth birthday celebration of the
Minnesota Vikings.

I was Entertainment Director for the Minnesota Vikings, on the field nine hours every gameday. And from that came a world record. Most times a marching band took the field and even that was pretty much already organized by the previous and continuing half-time director, Red McLeod.

What I brought to the position was that two of the half-times would now be huge, including the Vikings Twenty-fifth Birthday, and another, putting MDT's *Nutcracker* on the field. This time I did not have a street to overfill but I did have a giant grass stage. I loved the energy of my guaranteed large and energetic crowd.

My plan: to put an enormous danceline around the edge of the field. I recruited. The response from area dancelines was so large we could place them around the field, one girl per yard line, but also create a triangle on each end of the field. And each triangle pointed to—two purple and gold marching bands—who themselves formed the shape of the number "25"—and played Happy Birthday. And that might have come off perfectly.

BIG!

I ordered balloons for the crowd, to blow up and pop on cue. Popped balloons can't find their way to the field—I was trying to think of everything.

I love events that no one could imagine. How would the popping sound? I should have thought longer.

And then I noticed a record had been set for the World's Longest Chorus Line. Our girls will kick!

Record to Break:

The 1986 Guinness book had early Ziegfeld Follies with 120 girls. The previous book, 1985, showed a photo of 332 top-hatted strutters on a stage at the end of *A Chorus Line*, the longest-running Broadway show ever. And the Rockettes were also pictured at Radio City Music Hall in New York City, in a line regularly consisting of thirty-six.

Our Record:

Guinness told me that I set "accidental records," and I loved that. We went colossal for our own reasons, which didn't mean we didn't party in the name of Guinness! Into the 1987 book they went, the 516-member Minnesota Vikings birthday danceline, in a photo that covered half a page—huge—the largest we'd had yet—with the heading: "Longest off-stage chorus line."

The dancers came from schools in the area, and were costumed in NFL colors. They rehearsed at Vikings headquarters but were to have just one dome rehearsal.

At the start of halftime, the announcer called out the towns and their high schools, to the roar of the crowd:

"Mounds View, Rosemount, Richfield, Fridley; Totino Grace, Park Center, Brooklyn Park, Osseo; Minneapolis Edison, Minneapolis South, Columbia Heights, Coon Rapids; St. Paul Harding, Mound-Westonka, Osseo, Benilde-St. Margaret's; Robbinsdale Armstrong, Plymouth, Stillwater, Wayzata—and the St. Louis Park Parkettes!"

The big danceline performed seven routines, including a domino-like fall-down that started from two corners simultaneously; a mimed tap-dance to "Anything Goes" (on artificial turf), and a giant kick-line that ended with seventy-two kicks. The two purple marching bands came from Minneapolis Southwest and Brooklyn Center. They played "Happy Birthday"; the crowd blew up, waved, swayed and popped 62,145 balloons.

BIG!

The World's Longest Chorus Line surrounds two marching bands forming the number "25," for the twenty-fifth birthday of the Minnesota Vikings. (Thomas Obermeyer. Photo selected for the *Guinness Book of World Records*)

It sounded like as many back-firing motorcycles, in answer to our curiosity, although I've never heard 62,145 back-firing bikes.

At the end, the Vikings first pro-cheerleaders, Sue Anderson their coach, lay flat on the field, forming the number "'61-'85," the dates of the twenty-five years of the Vikings. The dash between the numbers was seven-year-old Lucia Lynn, daughter of Vikings General Manager Mike Lynn and his wife, Jorja. She gave the half-time an unexpected moment of suspense. Seven or seventy-seven years-old, it was impossible to read the numbers made by the cheerleaders from ground level. Lucia spun through them like a bee, searching. The cheerleaders cheered her on and she dropped, the dash, into place. Jorga watched her baby, through binoculars from the press box. But Lucia went into Barbara's column, a tiny star of the story of the spectacle.

It was scary to do an event this big as a half-time because game day was really always about football. We could not trip on the thousand wires on the sidelines; they belonged to coaches and television. We couldn't run late; the game was nationally televised. We couldn't distract the players just before or after. In my dreams I recruit football players to demonstrate passing a football, fancy, in front of the curtain at the opera, at intermission. Imagine.

So what went wrong? Not one but four stories on this event, nothing that ruined the event, just—the unexpected! Out-takes from events are at the end of the book, perhaps the best part, certainly educational for one planning even a small event.

Challenge:

A football fan wrote Guinness to say that the Vikings did not play on the date listed in the book; thus there could be no half-time birthday party.

Unfortunately, he was right. It did not happen on the date I listed. I was mortified but it was explainable, which never counts. I had two enormous events a week apart, this and the United Way half-time, and I mistakenly sent the United Way half-time date. The date was corrected in the next book.

Eventually, the Guinness book changed: the category: "Only chorus line records on a theatre stage will be considered." They listed the Ziegfield record and the *A Chorus Line* finale.

Sponsored by: The Minnesota Vikings

20

Leapfrogging in Frogtown

Frogtown, St. Paul, is a traditional city neighborhood with a rich busy history, near the Minnesota state capitol. It prides itself in its ethnic diversity. Bill Sands, president, Western Bank, in the Frogtown neighborhood, called me with the idea and off we went. Anyone leapfrog? My first yes: the mayor of St. Paul, James Scheibel. The bank became leapfrog central. With so much commotion the bank provided a locked meeting in which we could organize.

The athleticism of leapfrogging did limit interest, so we offered another option, a ceremony. The word "leapfrog" was painted in script on a thirty-foot by ninety-foot piece of red vinyl, to be covered by leapers. (The vinyl squares were borrowed from a United Way half-time.)

Record to Break:
Distance: 996.2 miles by fourteen students from Trancas dormitory at Stanford University, California. They leapfrogged 244 hours, forty-three minutes.

That did not sound fun or even possible for anyone, but certainly not for us. I asked for rules. The Guinness book responded. The Stanford distance record would no longer be a category and they gave us rules for a

BIG!

Above and right: leapfrog rehearsal at the West Minnehaha Recreation Center. (Beth Obermeyer, with permission of Julie Causey, chair, Western Bank, St. Paul)

leapfrog race instead. The new listing would be for the fastest pair to leapfrog over a mile. That we could do! We rehearsed, by their rec center.

The leapfrog trials went on all day. Kids and parents and business people stayed with it and we did get some great race times. Frogtown knew how to party. The winners—all from Jackson School—and the list of groups, a phone book of the world, included:

Age 12-14: Troy Randle and his cousin Josh Hernandez, 13:23;
Age 9-11: Stephanie Johnson and her sister McCall Johnson, 15:15;
Age 5: Crystal Larson and Andrea Carol-Fronk, 28:28

Also leapfrogging the word "Frogtown" on the thirty-foot vinyl square: SE Asian Ministry, Rock of Ages Missionary Baptist Church, Vietnamese Catholic Ministry, Calvary Evangelical Congregational Church, St. Stephanus Lutheran Church, among others; Women of Nations/Eagles Nest, Wilder Foundation, Hmong, Lao and American Translation Services; Yang See Travel Center; Hmong financial, grocery, medical services; dozens of Vietnamese bakery and grocery stores and restaurants. The day's entertainment included: The

Criminals from Ryan Plumbing; Triumphant Choir; Indian Drum/Dance; the Steele Family.

Our Record Filed: Finally the answer came: "We can only confirm that although we will keep this information on our files for future reference, we will be unable to publish the details in the book until we have received a number of comparable claims."

Decades passed. No further race frogleaping claim was entered. But the mayor showed how important the effort was: the *Pioneer Press* pictured him on page one as he made a giant athletic leap with the neighborhood.

The *ka-boom, ka-boom, ka-boom* of leapfrog thuds still can be heard, the beat of the area.

Sponsored by: The Frogtown Neighborhood Association, St. Paul.

St. Paul Mayor James Scheibel leapfrogging in Frogtown. (Richard Marshall. Reprinted with permission of *St. Paul Pioneer Press*)

21

The Mass Break Dance

7,000+, along the Mississippi River, in front of the St. Paul YWCA

Record to Break:
There was no record for a mass break dance. Break dance was a new phenomenon.

Diane Norman, who had been PR at the dance theatre, was now Director of PR at the St. Paul YWCA. And that was how I got there. I was thrilled to work with her again, and with Pepsi Cola as sponsor. What would be a good image event for the Y?

I thought break dancing, in front of the Y, the women's Y. Break dance was mostly done by young males. We would hire break dancers to teach it to everyone the Y served—seniors, families, young women or men. The idea exploded.

If I didn't already know the draw of those break dancers I did soon, and from an unlikely source: my mother. Home at Christmas, I showed my family my best videos of kids break dancing, reminiscent of period tap styles. I took a break, went upstairs to get a coke. Someone was in the kitchen. I heard brushing, swishing.

I tripped on my mother, now seventy-six! She was spinning on her back, legs tucked, eyes huge. "Wow," I said.

"I wanted to see if I could," she said, like she was about to pour coffee. That told me we were not wrong: the interest in break dancing would not be limited to young boys and men.

But back in St. Paul, well into auditioning break dancers to teach and help demonstrate, Guinness came down on us. "Break dance is too new, too special, to draw any competitive tries." It would not be a world record. Meanwhile, across town, the YMCA, the men's Y, overwhelmed with inquiries, posted a sign on their door: "Mass break dance not here! It's at the YW."

What we knew by then, anyway, was that the event was growing faster in numbers than we might be able to manage. We did not need the push of a Guinness record. We needed to settle down and manage the thousands of kids we already had, break dancing. And keep the seniors in their midst. The mix of young adolescent boys and girls was—I have no word for what it took for us to manage that. A benefit of not being with Guinness: we would not need to count them or get their signatures. We could just fill our eyes, and enjoy.

The Y flooded with people wanting to learn the dance; we hired twelve instructors, ages sixteen to twenty-six. Diane and I went, with our husbands, to First Avenue where Prince's dancers were featured. We targeted their establishment with flyers. These were the pros on that stage, our stars.

Our make-shift stage on the street—two pick-up trucks back to back—and it worked—got a smooth top surface. John Linnerson, Minnesota Dance Theatre, taped MDT's rolled flooring over the splinters.

The day came. Families, seniors, break dancers, teens, children, everyone filled the space between the stage and the river. Police were everywhere but we had no problems. Except Diane and I felt we were closer to catastrophe than we wanted to be, despite our planning. It just looked volatile.

But the dancers and the Y put it out there as planned. Act after act took the stage, the youngest, solo and groups; the teens; the seniors. The *St. Paul Pioneer Press* photo nailed it in one of their photos. Side by side—with an enormous crowd pulling for them—three dancers jived: an elderly agile-enough silver-haired woman; an awesomely large male dancer from Prince's *Purple Rain* film, stunning; and a young woman born in Hawaii, majored in political science at the University of Minnesota.

Tony Mosley, dancer in the film *Purple Rain*; Sylvia Brennan; and Gretchen Schnieder teach Mass Break Dance at the YWCA, St. Paul. (Joe Rossi. Reprinted with permission of *St. Paul Pioneer Press*)

The break dancers we hired to teach and the crowd leaders selected included: Johnnie "Electric Boogie Breaker" Young; Cliff "Don Juan" Alexis; Jonathan "Kicks-Ville Breaker" Wright; Gretchen "Sugar Pop" Schneider; Mark "Flash" Arias; Tony "Tutone" Mosley and Damon Dickson; The Heartbreakers; U.K. Breakers; Everette "Nature Boy" Kimbrough; Break Dance Boys, "Bam Bam" Lyell; P-Patrol; Circuit Breakers, Tony Gallahue; Mark Sunberg; Sonic Breakers; Yero Russell; Twin City Breakers; Marcus Jackson; BB Breakers; and David Germain.

And if my mother was interested, so was my daughter, now fifteen. I spotted her in the crowd with her friend Debbie Lazar, jiving near the front. They both had a crush on Johnnie Electric "Boogie Breaker Young" (as did a few thousand others.)

We did not file a record with the Guinness book. Many years later a record was in the book, far smaller than ours. We were ahead of our time and we had no Internet to create flash spectacles!

Big!

The challenge of managing thousands of break dancers was huge, it still freezes me. Going for Guinness would have tripled it. We did provide locked rooms to store boom boxes.

Soon after a department store had a break dance demonstration, in the store. Kids climbed the displays so they could see, damaged merchandise. I think it was because the crowd was all kids, no families, no seniors, no one to make them feel grounded. I can't believe the young people went home happy either.

Our break dancers had incredible energy and were so loved by all.

Interestingly, within months, our break dancers went from being arrested in the skyways of St. Paul—a nuisance—to reigning in our hearts—our American Idols of the streets.

22

The First Minnesota Festival of the Book

Not a record breaker, not at all. But . . . huge. Celebrating books for a week statewide counts, the vision of Scott Walker, Graywolf Press. And for me personally, it changed my life.

One day, three days before Christmas, I got a call to interview: Director, manager, the title seemed interchangable.

I arrived with bells on. This event would access my journalism side. I couldn't help but be keyed.

My idea at the interview: 100 authors—in "I Am an Author" buttons. Think: the event was to be on streets statewide. I was just handed it, one of those events. The Friends of the St. Paul Public Library shined with gems: Leslie Wolfson had toured book festivals nationwide. Mary Ida Thomson, president of the Friends of the St. Paul Public Library, had her following well in hand, including by then me.

Edie Meissner was a love of an administrator. And Susan Eilertsen, at her Word of Mouth PR company, had big publisher-author experience, from her previous position for a major publisher on the east coast.

The rich reality was that our Twin City area had a mine of small publishers, and more reading groups than hot dishes. The site for the opening was Disney-ish. Landmark Center, St. Paul, would be our castle, Rice Park, like a 1900 movie set, lay in front.

Big!

I knew full well how to make this mission visual, accessible to—everyone. I'd have kids explain, interpret their painted phrases on skateboards (as well as any graffiti they cared to share.) Bedtime stories in a big bed in the park. Librarians wanted to push carts with used books.

Sometimes great ideas can't make it out of committee, but not this time. Judy Geck, a third-generation bookstore pro, was the opening event volunteer chair. By the first meeting Paul Hannaman had ads guaranteed to push our librarians and authors to stardom. "It's a success waiting to happen," is what I said.

The week-long event for the people, everyone, ended with a Minnesota Book Awards. That first one was comparable to the excitement over the Oscars. Rosie O'Brien was chair.

I found a band made up of book critics; my contact was Dave Wood, book writer at the *Minneapolis Star Tribune*. A librarian sang "Marian the Librarian" from *The Music Man*. Garrison Keillor took part. Like that. No one exactly asked me to do this, but I tap danced to LeRoy Anderson's "The Typewriter" at the closing event, the first Minnesota Book Awards. It was a quick piece. The rhythm of the carriage *zinged* across, *dinged* back.

But mostly what I heard was the steps of the first winners of the Minnesota Book Awards, given that night. Thomas McGrath for *Collected Poems*, Patricia Hampl for *Spillville*, Barbara Juster Estbensen for *Star Maiden*, Gary Paulsen for *Hatchett*, Kathleen Coskran for *The High Price of Everything*, and Garrison Keillor for *Leaving Home*.

Lightning struck: I had a journalism degree, and I wasn't even reading. Or writing! Backstage, I told Scott I wanted to write. What did I want to write? I didn't know. He gave me a book on writing by Brenda Ueland. And that sounded like the start of a story, not the end.

Two decades later, just one month ago, I signed my first book for readers. The pencil scratched; I heard a rhythm in each name. I tapped the rhythm under the table. Now I wear tap shoes to signings. I've worn the letters off my laptop keyboard four times, more rhythms. And I don't even have to take the stage. I did not see that coming.

Epilogue

Under Our Feet

My parents didn't have to keep me off dangerous streets. I was a tap dancer, growing up in the town of *The Music Man*, for cripes sake. Or, as Meredith Willson liked to say, I was just "organizing my rhubarb." I was "dancing out" almost every night, pre-television, in a town that served up live entertainment like dessert. In Mason City, Iowa I could dance in the parks, or on a floating stage on Clear Lake, even two flat-bed trucks backed together. And yes, right on the street, or upon a platform at Farmers' Round-Up.

Proof is on celluloid, the finale of that film, The Music Man. The entire town floods onto the streets, from out the doors of the high school, singing "76 Trombones." They prance, whirl, slosh side-to-side like a tide of water, not a traffic cop in sight.

And then I married. I moved to the metropolis two hours north. I still remember seeing the city lights the first time, at night, driving in on 35W. Now I owned a skyline, protecting so many paths I needed a map. We dwelled in St. Paul for awhile, then settled by a lake path in Minneapolis. We could walk the sidewalks to downtown to work.

And did I hear the scuttlebutt. Just in case, never ever go where I could not be seen. (Now why would I do that?) Some streets, it was said, were dangerous. And did I know where mine was: I tap-danced six stories up from it, in the newly renovated Hennepin Center for the Arts, on Hennepin Avenue. But when I looked down from my skyscraper, I saw people stream on their sidewalks, pulse around corners, scoot across streets.

I imagined pouring puddles of paint on those sidewalks. Let the people strut through, criss-cross footprints at intersections, mark their routes. Lay claim. A Technicolor "Family Circus" cartoon.

And then the escapades began. Guinness records got set on that street and more intersections, by tap dancers to break dancers; leap froggers to bucket passers, through downtowns and neighborhoods, St. Paul to Minneapolis.

Don Del Fiacco, *St. Paul Pioneer Press*, finally summed it up: "She's gregarious, attractive, a mother of two . . . (she) lives quite grandly in the Kenwood district . . . (but, she) enthusiastically prowls our cities busiest thoroughfares . . . (the ones) once ruled quite elegantly by strippers Kandy Kane, Smokey Turner and Lisa Depraved!" I was busted.

My parents did not get that paper.

And that just didn't matter because the words were fast obsolete. The image of the thoroughfare blurred. Even the police joined the dance.

But here is the killer: many more large-scale people events now pop worldwide. The 1,801 tappers were ahead of the times, the first tap flash mob, staged long before the internet could help spread the word.

Flash mobs, so quick and easy.

The Internet changed the game, how we spread the word about anything. While we used stamps and the phone thirty years ago, a click now spreads information from Facebook to Twitter, our blogs go from Amazon Author Central to a website.

But even though the gathering of the people has simplified, the groundwork still must be laid. Just because the work is cut short, the organizer should not be tempted to click without thinking.

Tips for a great event can't change; they are whoppers to their success. I can cull them from the big event stories. Consider:
- A concept still needs to be able to be told—in one sentence. Picture the words on a billboard. We have seconds to understand.
- We still need to like our idea, be passionate. One wants to hear "You won't believe what I did today, or heard today."

- An idea still has to have a message. Everyone show up at midnight to open umbrellas . . . (It might rain?) Or everyone show up in tap shoes to open an arts center? (We all own the arts.)
- Be prepared: a fresh idea is open to more analysis than most. And warned: magic does not stand up to scrutiny. It's not easily sorted into a formula. "Creativity requires the courage to let go of certainties." (Erich Fromm)

  The flip side: if the idea is generic, one does not earn the right to start the flyer with "Imagine . . ." Therein lies the magic that makes us drunk.
- Important: bear in mind before you tweet: does the concept suit the client? Tie in your client, tight. Sponsor recognition is critical. Serve the client's ice cream outdoors in December. Who wouldn't report that?
- Have confidence in your idea but be ready to change direction. This might be hard to spot when the event comes together quickly, using the internet.
- Don't get hung up on criticism. Respond if you must but remember how far it goes with a click of a key. When one strikes back it goes to friends of dogs of societies of nations.
- Do think hard: what could go wrong? You are liable. Layer everything three times over to watch for Murphy's Law. Try a mini-version of the event and see what happens. If something goes wrong, it can go around the world quicker than a flicker.
- Don't panic. Answer three questions:

  Is someone going to get hurt?

  Will it ruin the event?

  If it happens, will the audience know the difference?

  That kind of stay-on-your-feet adjusting is timeless.
- Have an itemized list of what you expect to happen every five minutes so that if something happens you can see what it affects.

But events are not the only thing affected by the Internet. The Internet has even affected tap dance itself. For one, we thought tap was indigenous and unique to America, our own dance. Now many other countries lay claim to the origins of tap, based on their early drum rhythms. We can watch them on U-Tube. We can google mass tap-dance records and see dozens, sometimes 35,000 at a time!

Today, as never before, tap has many loyal followings, in at least a dozen different styles. Savion Glover says his style is hitting, and he likens his tap on his shoe to a drum surface with multiple angles and ways of striking. Irish dancers say their style is stepping. Paul Draper believed his classical tap based on ballet was superior.

How is tap taught when there are so many styles? Back to the way it was taught in the beginning.

Master the basics, then listen and watch, whether in a studio or on the Internet.

Mimic; steal and trade.

The Hoofer's Club in Harlem had a fast rule: "Thou shalt not copy anyone's steps—exactly! Look and listen—copy, yes—but creatively modify. Today we can quickly access tap on U-Tube, on websites, watch steps over and over. Tap dancing is for everyone, like never before.

But think up this: if tap can expand in any direction since it combines visual with sound, a percussive music, does that not make tap cutting edge?

Soon, the Cowles Center for Dance will open on Hennepin Avenue, end of 2011. The Cowles is a theatre that was moved on wheels down Hennepin, so large it set a Guinness record for the largest building ever moved over a block. Renovated, it now rests, attached to the Hennepin Center for the Arts.

Flash mobs will show up. Photos of the 1,801 tappers will reign in the Cowles lobby, a nod to the past. And tap dancers will be a proud and important part of the Cowles season—Savion Glover, the protégé of Gregory Hines; and Buckets & Tap Shoes, a young exciting local troupe, gone international. We're all in our places, a circle of sorts, around and back.

Wheels of our lives move forward, overlap, slide back, in a loop, it seems.

Once one dances, one must always dance, I think.

Most tap on wood. Some on concrete.

You can even tap on ice, probably. How about on a cloud?

I think we just did.

Big!

Because when we pulled together—BIG—we became more alike than different.

And that may be the biggest dance of all.

Out-Takes and Hind Sights:
So What Went Down?
A Scramble to Fix

T he tales, the legends, the lessons—event and tap—are over, and it's time to close the story. But not before the ripple of Out-Takes. Because how was it, how was it, really?

I never hear . . . please brag about what went right. But . . . what really went down? Then what? Could anyone have prevented it?

And some Out-Takes aren't chaos at all, but just interesting challenges that were solved.

Herein lies all the years of event experience, the kind one learns from a sense of how unexpected live entertainment can be—and how to hold steady and work through. Because a one-of-a-kind event is worth a million.

And I'm not telling tales here on anyone. Sometimes a live event—so rare today with all the editing skills and photo shopping—the real thing—can surprise and startle. In one moment the event can go as blameless as a Laurel and Hardy segment: stuff just happens when everything comes together.

Like out-takes at the end of a Dean Martin show, some details are hilarious in retrospect. All the same, they happened.

So here it comes: the pandemonium we didn't predict.

It's tell me a story . . . Tell me a story . . . Tell me a story . . . Especially about the monkeys please . . .

1. **Don't Rain on my Violin.** Fifty children from MacPhail Arts Center were invited to be a marching violin unit in a parade; they accepted. But—we soon realized why we had not seen a marching violin unit before. What if it rained? They'd have to stay home. Just the sun was hard enough on wood. They couldn't sit in damp grass in line-up, either. They had to learn not only to march but also to start and stop. Turn corners. From MacPhail Center for the Arts, they were as young as three. But disciplined—amazing—all fifty, and well worth the adjustments. Event: Debut: Aquatennial, Sponsor WCCO-TV special unit.

Three-year-old marching violinist at the MacPhail Center for the Arts. (Mike Paul. Courtesy of HOT CHA! Parade, *Minneapolis St. Paul Magazine* and WCCO-TV)

2. **Fifty Boys and Girls with Bats.** What a Visual: The Kaleidoscope, a Pre-Parade show, filled a downtown intersection. Five concentric circles of 236 children—gymnasts, fruits, dancers—were ready to tumble, cavort, dance, spin lariats for overhead cameras. But the outside circle was fifty Little Leaguers connected hand to bat to hand. But unlike dancers and gymnasts, the batters had nothing to practice but—bat swinging? Answer: they'll sit cross-legged, bats on the

ground—two feet away—until the Metropolitan Boys Choir sings, the cue. Event: WCCO-TV, Aquatennial Parade

3. **Snow White's Not Talking.** (same event) The centerpiece of the concentric circles was the real Snow White. My son, Mark, nineteen, was a help, placing the vinyl; but after he slumped. "Mom, she's a babe but she won't talk to me. I had some good stuff." "Who?" I asked. "Maybe," I said, "it's because you called her a babe?" "Snow White," he said. "And she's in so much dress, poufy skirt and sleeves as big as her head. It's like bumper cars with a marshmallow." I explained with care: "She can't talk, she is in character. Mark, it's a costume." Mark had spent the last half hour trying to spend time with Snow White, everyone's fantasy I suppose. Nothing I could say made sense to him. She was pretty.

4. **Let the Festivities Begin!** It was time to start. I ran for my bagpiper. But who knew the glass door—where he was warming-up—locked when closed? I pounded but he couldn't hear over the pipes. Hundreds of performers hung in place. Edina Mayor C. Wayne Courtney was ready—to go to the next event, that is. We could have had a flautist. Finally the piper turned, saw me doing my traffic-stopping dance. In the end? No one knew what happened: the show went on. Event: Ground-Breaking Ceremony, Edinborough

5. **Bring in the Clowns!** I led sixty clowns through the Metrodome, dropped one clown off in each aisle, to pass out balloons, 60,000 balloons in 600 buckets. But they would only answer my directions in clown jokes; they mimed my every move, because they were—clowns. I couldn't read their expressions or their eyes. Up in the press booth, the dome still empty, I watched them run the aisles, like balls in a slot machine. But on cue, the crowd got their balloons, blew them up and popped them—not something I could have rehearsed. Awesome. Event: Minnesota Vikings Twenty-Fifth Birthday.

6. **The Football Team and the Dancers.** Same event. The 516 danceline girls sat on the Dome floor, the length of the field, close behind the players in places. Distracting! said the visiting NFL team. The headset landed on my head. Move them! said Merrill Swanson, from up in the PR booth. My prob-

lem: the girls were sitting in order of their entrance. I needed a ¾ mile long tunnel for line-up. Tunnels around sport venues were called vomitoriums in gladiator days; staying lined up there wasn't an option. I strung them on either end of the field, sat them three deep, hoped they'd remember their order. On cue, they took four minutes to run the perimeter of the field; they started. They pulled it off.

7. **Let the Music Begin** . . . Same event. The girls entered in one stream. They danced, the balloons popped, but the band director did not start Happy Birthday. Make music no one can hear? It was the director's dilemma. Time ran down. As the girls started to run off, the music started (why many half-times are pre-recorded—no matter what happens, the main parts will go on and the live parts will insert themselves.) But no one knew the difference. No one could have predicted how long 60,000 balloons would take to pop.

8. **He's Standing on Top of a Water Fountain.** It was Friday before Monday's concert. I drove-by. Peavey Fountain had not been drained for the winter. The emcee and soloists were to stand atop this fountain. City crews don't work on week-ends. A call to the city and the fountain was drained. It might have happened anyway but it never hurts to check. Event: World's Largest Marching Band; Downtown Council/Greater Minneapolis Chamber of Commerce

9. **They're Playing in Fumes.** Same event: the biggest band rehearsal, Peavey Plaza outside Orchestra Hall. Buses dropped-off in the drive (permission had been granted,) pausing to unload. But bus fumes entered the air system of Orchestra Hall; musicians inside became ill enough to stop their rehearsal. Of course by then we were finished un-loading.

10. **Doughboy Direct.** Same event. The Pillsbury Doughboy led The World's Marching Band eight blocks, from the rehearsal to the Pillsbury-sponsored picnic. On the way he was to stop outside Pillsbury headquarters for a short band concert. But the Doughboy took a shorter, more direct route to the picnic. He probably couldn't see. Or—perhaps it was because the Doughboy doesn't go to work every day?

11. **And the Exit Is?** Same event. To simplify the exit from picnic to march, a site map was marked to show where each band was to sit; but the thirty-three big number cards and bricks to weight—to mark their spots—didn't get placed, bad story; and so the bands landed anywhere. Line-up got tricky—bands walked through bands to get in the order of march, like syrup from where I stood. Every job is important; a risk when not done.

12. **Vehicles over Fourteen Feet Tall Prohibited.** Same event. A parking location map for buses was mailed to all band directors. One director called: the ramp he was to park in was not tall enough at the entrance for the bus. He was right. And it was an easy fix, ahead.

13. **Bands Don't Litter.** Same event. In my dream the night before, 2,500+ musicians are sticking large paper bibs to each other's backs, as planned. But as they ripped off the two-foot square backing papers, thousands of papers floated in the wind, like giant confetti. The band marched—left it all behind, captured by TV cameras in helicopters. I woke up, realizing I needed ten bag people by that night to pass trash bags down 167 rows of band, and collect the bib backings.

14. **Tap Dancing on Nails.** It was parade day, raining, pouring; tappers were about to set the world distance record, the lead two in foam board Minneapple costumes. But the glue holding the shoulder braces will let go when wet. Tom fashioned clear plastic raincoats for the giant red apples. But the rain soaked the leather soles of the tap shoes and the nails in the taps wiggled against our feet. We danced less and walked more. But there were two parades. Next time. Event: The Minneapple; Josh Levinson, owner.

15. **Dancers Prefer Football, not Baseball.** It's the World's Longest Chorus Line rehearsal; but the field of the Metrodome was marked for baseball, not the ten-yard lines for football that the girls expect, rely on. We re-created the lines with ribbons, anchored by duct tape; it was fragile but worked for the rehearsal. The unexpected advantage: the girls were subsequently asked not to dance on the actual field lines at their performance because fifteen minutes of pounding would wear them off for the football team. Event: Minnesota Vikings Twenty-fifth Birthday.

16. **Babies Bawl by Dinnertime.** On a cool fall morning, the client put its heated floor product in a thirty-foot by thirty-foot playpen, a Playpen Olympics. But it was a convention and morning is good speaker time. The Olympics was changed to 5:30 p.m. Now I needed babies with naps and parents who are already in the car at 5 p.m. Head Start! The client paid for the bus and donated fifty dollars per baby. Event: Gyp-Crete's Billionth-Square-Foot of Poured Flooring Celebration.

17. **It Never Snows in Southern Minnesota** . . . It's December: a snow sculpture contest of Nutcracker characters was planned. It didn't snow. We scrambled. The tap dancers do a Snow Dance down the Nicollet Mall. But Munsingwear gives us fabric; we change to Nutcracker Fabric Sculptures. For Bridgeman's it was a Forbes Magazine Business in the Arts Award and a 1981 Minneapolis Mayor's Public Art Award. Event: Bridgeman's Ice Cream Parlour's Night at the Nutcracker; through Campbell Mithun's Group Five.

Snow Dance, Bridgeman's Loring Park Nutcracker. (Reprinted permission of *Star Tribune*)

18. **The United Way Out.** A half-time can have thousands of people. Marilyn Nelson, CEO of The Carlson Companies, was a woman with an idea, for the United Way: the UW could be a half-time. Soon we had Bob Jani, The Super Bowl King, Director; and L.A. choreographer, Miriam Nelson. When finished here she would do the Mary Martin Show in San Francisco.

Something big was on its way. The concept would duplicate the white United Way poster, which showed a green stem with red blossoms and the title "Love Makes a Difference." And so the field was covered with thirty ten-yard square pieces of red vinyl, reversible to white—or 3,000 square yards. On top of the flipping vinyl, all red, all white, checked red and white, were dancers with ribbons. Until the end when hundreds of UW volunteers in white hooded tops and white pants and white shoes would go into posi-

United Way Half-time, "Love Makes a Difference." (Photo courtesy of United Way; A Bob Jani Production; Minnesota Vikings Half-time; Metrodome, Minneapolis)

tion and out of white bags pull red and green pom poms to create the image of the stem and blossoms. If ever there was a United Way it was this, done to Charlie Title's original music: "Love Makes a Difference."

And it was evident from the earliest rehearsals that we were tied together. If the vinyl didn't flip on time, the dancers went splat. If the vinyl lined up incorrectly on the sideline to start, the pattern would not be correct for the stem and flower. Paul Ridgeway reigned throughout the logistics. And then the Out-Take I remember most. The cast was stored in a nearby armory, to walk to the Metrodome for half-time. The weather forecast: rain. The solution? Bring a trash bag, poke holes for the eyes, stay dry to the dome. On cue, thousands of dry United Way volunteers would drift, armory to metrodome, through the tunnels, towards the tiny black dots on the vinyl that mark the 1,000 yard-tall stem and flower, just like the UW Poster. I don't even remember if it rained, just the image of thousands of UW volunteers hiking in trash bags is enough. Event: United Way—Minnesota Vikings Half-Time; "Love Makes a Difference."

19. **Sleeping with Pom Poms.** Same Event. Trade secret: pom poms do not arrive fluffed; they look like shimmery hula skirts. Solution: crimp them. Squish with fists and stuff them under a mattress, overnight. Repeat. Until smashed, crinkly to sparkle. Our 2,000 United Wayers had some of the finest pom poms, the best.

20. **Green in 1984.** Same Event. I borrowed the ten-yard square red-vinyl pieces often: for a thirty-foot square crossword puzzle that opened the first Minnesota Festival of the Book; for Children's Book Week, different clues; for Iowa State University where I was a Professional in Residence. Several pieces of the vinyl went to the Frogtown Festival to be a red base for the massive leapfrogging. One piece covered a downtown intersection for WCCO-TV's Aquatennial pre-parade show. Hundreds of pom poms went to the Vikings 25th Birthday party. Tired of the back and forth, the keeper of pom poms and vinyl at the United Way finally asked: Beth. Can't you store these at your house? Yes. (Four squares, folded, a five-foot tall stack.)

21. **Bankers and Numbers.** I taught a twenty-part routine to bank employees for a parade. Five minutes into the rehearsal, the Norwest bankers shouted the count, pivoted, and snapped off moves. The next year it was First

Bank: in no time bells and cards whipped and thumped to the count. Conclusion: bankers make smart parade units, take to numbers and rhythms. Event: Norwest Bank (with cards;) First Bank (with bells and flakes;) St. Paul Winter Carnival Parade

22. **Cooler than Mary Tyler Moore.** Mary Tyler Moore came back to downtown Minneapolis to throw her hat in the air, as she did for the promo for The Mary Tyler Moore Show. She had no idea how cool it could be in Minnesota. A small woman shivering was hard to watch. We loaned her a coat. Event: Twentieth Birthday of the Nicollet Mall, Minneapolis; Downtown Council

23. **The Right Time, The Right Place. The Right People.** Same Event. Big. A mass hat toss by a couple dozen downtown celebrities, ones with history downtown. My job: get the celebrities there and direct the toss. The Nicollet

Nicollet Mall's Twentieth Birthday, Mary Tyler Moore Hat Toss. (Leo Kim; *The Directory* cover; Courtesy of the Downtown Council, Minneapolis)

Mall is twenty years old, a very big deal. The Downtown Council sent a longtime secretary. And their mascot and leaders. I added the ones I noticed—the popcorn lady, a musician, a bus driver. The key, I knew: make the time and place incredibly convenient for busy people. And so, a Sunday morning before a Vikings game it was—and the parking was provided. The photo I promised would take twenty to thirty minutes maximum, a half-dozen tosses. I delivered some of the hats personally first, bulldozed right up to the desks of some all-business executives. Café del-Arte promised breakfast. They accepted!

Barbara Carlson, City Council; Bob Dayton, The Conservatory partner; Phil Disch, the mall maintenance crew foreman; Charlotte Sunderlin, the mall popcorn lady; Tony Taylor, MTC bus driver; an itinerant whistler, frequents the mall; Barbara Flanagan, *Star*; Pat Lindquist, *Skyway News*; O.D. Gay, retired President, Downtown Council; Randy Lee Hendler, Sideshow Productions; Del Mar, musician; Maurice Adelsheim, Nicollet Mall Advisory Board Chairman; Judy Zaitz, twenty-year secretary, Downtown Council; Noah Freed, YWCA Children's Center; The Roosevelt Rockettes; SantaBear, Dayton's; Nicollet Bear, Downtown Council mascot; Mika Spasejovich, stand-in for woman on the MTM promo; Rev. Donald Meiser of Westminster Presbyterian Church. Event: *Directory,* published by Downtown Council

City lore: the celebration was loaded with history. Before Nicollet was declared a mall, Nicollet was a trail to Fort Snelling. When travelers crossed the Mississippi towards downtown Minneapolis, they either turned right at Goose Pond and headed to northern settlements or went left to Fort Snelling, on trails that became what is now Hennepin Avenue and Nicollet Avenue.

Some in *The Directory* magazine cover photo were descendants of, or the same as, those at the groundbreaking of the mall in 1966—including Barbara Flanagan; O.D. Gay; Bob Dayton. The Roosevelt Rockettes represented the reincarnation of Donaldson's (Golden Rule) at their new location (Donaldson's opened with the real Rockettes on the street.) Rev. Donald Meiser's church was on the street in 1887. Trivia: the woman off to the side of the hat tossers came from the office of *The Directory Magazine*, to represent the woman in the opening scene of the *Mary Tyler Moore Show*, who watches Mary in disbelief.

And that woman surfaced again in 1996. Her daughter brought her to the Mall of America for a Mary Tyler Moore book signing. Her name was

Hazel Frederick and she was by then ninety-one years old. Mary Tyler Moore introduced her to the crowd as her "co-star." On the day the show's opening credits were filmed Hazel had been shopping at Dayton's. She stood by the side, just wondering—what's going on?

24. **Her Job Is to Answer the Phone.** But now her phone rang continually. The St. Paul YWCA was planning a mass break dance and thousands of people of every age wanted to learn it. The Board of Directors loved seeing so many people want to participate. But the receptionist whose job it was to answer the phone? It's all added to her regular job and now—she hates the event and her job and me and even break dancers. Stand ready for wild success; they might call on the phone. Event: Mass Break Dance, YWCA, St. Paul

25. **Not on My Wood Floor You Don't—Tap Dance.** The school principal may love to have tap dancing taught in the school hallway in the evening but the janitor in charge of wood floors will not. He threatened to lock the doors. Tappers got moved to the lunchroom tile floor. Tap 'til drop—to the scent of milk. Event: Community Education; Adult tap

26. **They're Four Years Old.** 234 four-year-olds are to sing "The People on the Bus" for a transit station opening. Intuition said, in this much excitement—they will probably not be totally toilet-trained. I had the Head Start vans pull alongside the stage; the children performed on arrival, sang their song many times—on demand—and bused home quickly after. The crowd could hardly part with them. Yes, the stage floor got mopped here and there before the barefoot contemporary dancers took the stage, next. Event: Dedication: Sixth Street Transit Station; Hennepin Merchants Association

27. **Client Is Clear.** "Mostly I Need a Full-Size Elephant." Suepenn (Supatinasinkasem) at Sawatdee Thai Restaurant wanted a parade; that was my thing, no problem. I paused at understanding "Bressing at the Liver," (Blessing at the River,) understandably. (Even though my sister-in-law is Korean.) The consonants can get switched, going from one language to the next. But I am certain she says—"Elephant." Thai culture has great respect for elephants. I find a man with a ten-foot-tall one—in his front yard. We

Kids singing "The People on the Bus."

BIG!

Top: Sixth Street Transit Station Opening with 234 Head Start four-year-olds singing, "The People on the Bus." Bottom: Transit Station wrapped in Mr. Teener's bow, Teener Theatrical.

can have it if it's delivered it to his friend's front yard when finished. Perfect! Event: Sawatdee Thai Restaurant opening.

Elephant in procession to open Sawatdee Thai Restaurant. (Courtesy of *Skyway News*; Courtesy of Supenn S. Harrison, Sawatdee Thai Restaurant)

28. **The Band Plays On . . . Not.** A marching band was to start an important community event. They cancel day of—too early in the fall, no time to rehearse. Johnny Howard, emcee, started the back-up tape; it breaks. Neighbors crouch, waiting to start their dance, now sit, now sprawl. A parade of people wait. Mayor Jim Sheibel, set to lead, sends a note to a VFW across the street; their drum quartet saves the day. (Two times backed up wasn't enough; rule of thumb: three.) Event: Frogtown Festival, Opening.

29. **Trapped.** Rows of wagons were lined up for a parade, eight across, tied together in rows; a balloon company was filling them, each one. My job: to whistle start and stop them down the route. Make them dance, circle. But: yellow buses were parked around the entire block. We were hemmed in. A wagon brigade can't file out one wagon at a time; it had to head out an eight-wide wagon unit. Eventually, two side-by-side buses found their drivers and moved. Event: Aquatennial parade. For Robert Smith Events.

Stage Door dancers at International Market Square.

30. **Dancing on the Tables?** "Something sparkly for the guests." I called Sue Anderson. She had 100 dancers. The dance was to start around a balcony and proceed down a three-story circular stair, perform at the base. Our rehearsal started at the top. But beneath us—on our stage, the floor—were a dozen tables, set with crystal, china. Solution: Waiters rehearsed. They picked up set tables, backed up steps and placed them, out of the way, just in time for dancers to take the floor. After, the waiters stepped the tables back to the floor. It worked, even appeared choreographed. Event: International Market Square. Stage Door Dancers.

31. **The Building Can't Open.** Seven hundred trumpeters are invited to play an opening, outdoors. Downtowners will flock to tour the new skyscraper. But months passed and it was apparent: the building would not be finished by the opening date. The opening was postponed—to an indoor winter opening. A crowd was not likely to gather in cold; horns are difficult in the cold as well. The new building donated $50 for each horn player as planned, to

the marching bands of the 700 players. And: "Thank you; thank you. Thank you!" came back. Event: Norwest Bank Opening, downtown Minneapolis.

32. **Carol Bly Writes on Pizza Boxes.** A giant crossword puzzle, so large the letters were on pizza boxes. Carol Bly authored the literary puzzle. But when photo time came—Carol was not comfortable; it was hard to grin holding up pizza box letters, especially on command. The photographer opted to go up a level, took the photo overhead. Event: Minnesota Festival of the Book opening event.

33. **Crossed Boxes.** Could I do an event on my college campus as a Professional in Residence? I'll send a thirty-foot red vinyl square, for another crossword puzzle. But on that exact day my computer died. A new computer arrived, in two large boxes. And the dog died as well. We put the hound in one box, the heavy folded vinyl in the other. Daylight came. Tom mailed the vinyl to Iowa State. Back home he said the vinyl box—"really heavy. Sixty pounds." I said it: "Did you look inside the vinyl box before you mailed?" One box was mailed, the other was buried. We waited it out. We got it right. Event: PRSSA, Iowa State University, Ames, Iowa.

Crossword Puzzle Goes to Iowa State University, PRSSA (Public Relations Student Society of America). (Tom Emmerson)

34. **And She Said . . .** A reporter asked a question of ten-year-old Kristin, inside her Tapping Minneapple costume. "How does it feel to be dancing inside an apple?" "Like I've lost my marbles." Event: The Client (the understanding client): The Minneapple, Josh Levinson.

35. **Fifty+ Years Ago . . .** On the *Ted Mack Original Amateur Hour*, July, 1959, I was seventeen and my sister was that same age—ten. Mr. Mack asked: "And what do you want to do, Mary Beth?" "I'm going to go on to college, Mr. Mack." "And what are your plans, Julie?" "Oh, Mr. Mack, I just want to get married," Julie said. Ted Mack laughed and spun his wheel of fortune. "Well, if there are any ten-year-old bachelors out there, just dial . . ." Next, a Geritol ad: "If you've been feeling down and out, need a pick-me-up . . ."

36. **The Itinerant Tin Whistler.** I was Tapping Santa. My taped music echoed in the many-storied space. Unmanageable. So I danced a cappella. But a haunting whistle tune mysteriously bounced off the hard surfaces of the atrium, just right. I searched: behind a column, sat a character who appeared to be in costume but I thought he was not. I thought he might be homeless; at least he was unique. We went back and forth and it was eerie, beautiful, for hours, more dancing. He left but not until he scribbled on my paper: "Itinerant Tin Whistler." Event: Promotion; Butler Square.

37. **Tap-dancing on Ice on Radio.** A radio show was doing a closing ceremony for the Celebrity Dog-Sled Race. I called Sue Frase, the producer: I could organize 876 tap-dancing afghan hounds—and put them on ice, in front of Mickey's Diner in St. Paul. In tails. St. Paul's mayor, George Latimer came to the art deco beauty. We described the ceremony. I got the idea watching my own afghan hound react to sand at Lake Calhoun, skittering like it was ice. Event: *Boone & Erickson*, WCCO-AM.

38. **The Nutcracker Twist on Turf.** It was a great idea and it wasn't mine. The general concept was in place for the season before I arrived. The Vikings gave it to me because I knew dance needs. But the rehearsal of mice, soldiers and all stumbled, literally. The artificial turf was causing ankle injuries. The planted foot tended to stay and twist, even though dancing on pointe on turf was otherwise surprisingly superb. It was sad and curious at the same time to

see dancers fall down like football players do all the time. We all developed empathy for the football players. Event: Minnesota Vikings Half-Time; Minnesota Dance Theatre "Nutcracker Fantasy."

39. **Loony.** The Minnesota Loon was Grand Marshall of a parade, a six-foot-tall bird costume with a person inside. The resume arrived: Warbler Award for Claire de Loon; flies around the world from the Lindbird (Lindberg, now re-named) Terminal; spokesloon for the Department of Tourism. Much much more. Event: Summer Pleasures Parade, sponsored by WCCO-TV and *Mpls. St. Paul Magazine*.

40. **Different Loon.** Same event. A twenty-foot loon rode on a flat bed in the parade. It normally floated on Silver Lake; I realized it was larger than a bird pictured in the Guinness book. Sheila Colosimo, Virginia gave me a photo and I sent just that in, facts on the back of the card. 1989 book: the bird appeared as the World's Largest Decoy. But loons are not decoys said Jeff Fox, managing editor of the Virginia, Minnesota paper. "We don't get too technical about it," said Cyd Smith, asst. editor of the book. "I mean…a duck is a duck." Colismo: "That is a little bit inaccurate, but that is the category they had." If Guinness didn't already know about Minnesotans, their accuracy and truthfulness—they did soon. Their duck, the town declared, was definitely not a decoy. The entire category was dropped from the 1990 book.

Loon on Silver Lake, Virginia, Minnesota. (Gene L. Obryan; Courtesy of Laurentian Chamber of Commerce)

41. **I'll Have It My Way, the Lady Said.** It was a book festival, opening day, a welcome to 100 authors. Each was to sign a helium balloon on arrival, which was tied to a string of any length—ten feet to a hundred feet—with a metal washer weight on the bottom. The balloons on strings were placed in the many-storied atrium, a great visual. But a volunteer, no reason given, in a sudden sweep, pulled all of the strings together and twisted them into one. Perhaps the skittering of the balloons in the breeze seemed untidy to her. But do it she did and the balloon sculpture that had grown magnificently as the day went on—was over. Which was too bad because it didn't involve a balloon vendor, just volunteers blowing up balloons and tying them to strings, ingenious. But—did anyone arriving know the difference? No. But the beauty was diminished and the bunched balloons made the signatures unreadable. Any volunteer job, even one watching over balloons, can turn critical if they do something no one could have predicted. Event: A Book Affair; Minnesota Festival of the Book.

42. **Steve Schussler, an Event on His Own.** I'd done many events with Steve. We exploded the same amount of hoopla except—the main difference—I'm from Mason City, Music Man Iowa. He's from nine states east. *We put Mayor Fraser up in a cherry picker to direct 7,000 people with pom poms, fans who couldn't get into the Dome for the World Series. *For the second coming of the Twins World Series, I ask Dun-Rite Cleaners, across the street, to dry clean and press our Homer Hankies. *For the World Series parade, Steve goes to the Federal Reserve Bank and gets chopped money for confetti. Steve Schussler is a living Out-Take, always. Even in a parade of Out-Takes. Event: World Series Rallies, Jukebox Saturday Night, downtown Minneapolis.

43. **A Reunion of Mice and Flakes.** Loyce Houlton, artistic director, Minnesota Dance Theatre, wanted a twenty-sixth year reunion of her "Nutcracker Fantasy" and she contracted me to do it. My new project was nearly impossible: most of her records had been thrown; I had no mailing list. I made a Wanted Poster, for a soldier, a flake and a mouse. But dancers live all over the world. But by opening night, Darcy Pohland WCCO-TV, did introduce hundreds from the stage; they saluted in the aisles. At intermission they danced in a nearby space. Inspired and unexpected: photographers Conrad Razidlo, Myron Papiz, others, joined the round-up; they turned in so

many slides, prints that Tom did a lobby slide show. Loyce, startled and honored at the generosity of her loyal partners, months later, in her home, was able to touch through shoe boxes of slides and photos. Event: Twenty-sixth Reunion, "Nutcracker Fantasy."

44. **Your Summer Pleasure?** A parade of summer pleasures, through streets of downtown, struck a chord and went stellar, exponentially for a first-time parade. The mayor and city council came in cardboard tow truck, sander, cop car; community groups rejoiced. When it happens, and sometimes it can only happen once, magic is priceless:

Minneapolis Mayor Donald Fraser and City Council's Barbara Carlson, Hot Cha! Parade, WCCO-TV and *Mpls St. Paul Magazine.*

A Walking Corn Field (people with yellow balloons pinned in rows;) Sunglass and Squirt-Gun (ala Miami Vice;) Kenwood Perrier Marching Band (blowing partially filled bottles for music;) Inner Tube Troupe, Pinwheel Procession; Pancake Flipout; Sunflower Spitters; Out-house Racers; Party-to-go under Walking Tent; Caravan of Clouds; Country Kids with Blue Ribbons (and a cow;) Vern Gagne and The Big Boy Brigade. The Cast of Oklahoma, Singing. Event: HOT CHA! Parade, WCCO-TV and *Mpls St. Paul Magazine.*

45. **Happy Birthday Baby**! The Hennepin Center for the Arts turned 10. I delivered my exhibit of twenty-two framed photos, letters, awards, given to me by the Elayne Galleries, to be put on display at the arts center for the gala. I gave a speech on my memories of the opening, sure of its meaning by then. Reporting on creativity comes hard when it involves oneself; it's hard to know: how engaged is the listener? It's like a tap dance: take the stage, explode, take long bows and out.

BIG!

Beth leaping in front of Seventy-six Trombones. (Mike Paul; Courtesy of Gary Johnson; HOT CHA! Parade; *Mpls St. Paul Magazine* and WCCO-TV)